Here's what some synergy leaders have to
Turning Points: Journey

The Synergy Pals rekindle the rich spirit that
our lives, to explore the world from four points
to our own with those who matter most in wo

Jack Canfield and Mark Victor Hansen
co-authors, Chicken Soup for the Soul MEGA SERIES

In principle, science should be able to tell us what we ought to do to live the best lives possible.

Sam Harris, author, The Moral Landscape and The End of Faith

We are all different. Dr. Reverman has captured those differences in this work and made it easy and natural for child and adult to get back into the understanding mode, so that everyone in the family can be comfortable and accepted.

the late Lendon H. Smith, M.D., author, The Children's Doctor

Being emotionally fit gives you the strength to express your uniqueness. The Synergy Pals Profile is an easy personality assessment tool to enlighten and entertain while exploring human needs for relationship.

C.G. Cale, investment manager

A beginner's guide to the basics of understanding temperament roles. Both science and common sense show us our view of human intelligence is far too narrow; we ignore a crucial range of abilities that matter immensely in terms of how we succeed in life.

Douglas Houser,
attorney, Bullivant, Houser, Bailey, Pendergrass & Hoffman

The strength of the book is in the examples of how sensory styles interact in the real world. Different situations can threaten each of the personality types into different expressions of self-need and discord. Understanding the different ways people process information is an important skill we use all our lives.

Susan Hammer, attorney at law-mediator, and Lee Kelly, sculptor

What drives people…to be right, to be liked, to seek attention, to have control, to protect family and everyone you love. This book redefines what it means to be smart. One people living on one planet. This the first generation to be aware of ourselves as a WHOLE.

Tony Alessandra, Ph.D., NSA, author of The Platinum Rule

We support this effort to invest in children, the environment and peace to make a difference (of perception) in the world.

Nansie and Raymond G. Jubitz,
Executive Director, Jubitz Family Foundation

This Book Belongs To

_____

Friendly Universe Collection #2

Turning Points
Journey to Self Discovery

*Find the place
where our talents
and desires meet*

Ardys U. Reverman, Ph.D.

Illustrated by Charlotte Lewis

Copyright © 1995
Reprint 2011 by Ardys Urbigkeit Reverman
Published by
Friendly Universe Collection®
Printed in the United States of America

First edition 1995

Library of Congress Cataloging in Publication Data
Reverman, Ardys U.
Turning Points: Journey to Self Discovery
Summary: An adult/child interactive book to help children recognize and respect
the different ways people think, grow and view the world.
The Synergy Pals work as a team to redirect chaos.
p. 223 cm.
1. Self-respect. 2. Self-perception. 3. Success—Psychological aspects.
4. Personality development. 5. Temperament strengths.
6. Parental acceptance. 7. Cognition I Title. 8. Collaboration
I. Title.

BF801.R   1995
158.1   dc20   92—91277
                             CIP
ISBN 978-0-9625385-7-5

Visit us on the web at
www.synergypals.com
www.friendlyuniverse.com

We come from the roots of our grandparents' tree,
meaning-makers at the beginning of the new.

To my grandchildren, the growing branches
connecting us to the whole earth:
Caroline, Eloise, Anna, Amelia,
Ella, Alex Jr. and Cash.

Story

Somewhere in a galaxy not far away a story is being told.
It doesn't have a name yet. That is why it is referred to as Story.
But it knows that much of what it has been taught about learning and
teaching is wrong, and that is why it is on a quest.

It knows (and has known for a long time) that there are
beings in the universe who can hear it, sometimes faintly and
sometimes clear as a bell.

Once it popped into the head of a football coach when his team
was right on the opponents' goal line. He didn't pay attention
and Story didn't get through.

A few thousand years ago a baby was with its mother
by the side of a great river. It heard Story. Trouble was, the baby
couldn't speak yet, and Story got lost.

But it persisted!

It kept circling the Earth and popping into the noosphere.
Every few years it found more and more people who were curious,
who heard fragments and wanted more. Those people began to
meet each other and share thoughts, and they found that each of them
had a different part of Story. And to their surprise, as they delved deeper
and deeper into the parts they understood, they found Story there
in its entirety, waiting...

— Caine & Caine

Acknowledgments

My heartfelt thanks to others on the vanguard of this work, and from family and friends who, in living, walk life's journey in their own way. Creativity creates itself as we learn our living story is our brain food. What's extraordinary becomes ordinary during our journey of self discovery by exploring new ways of learning.

Thank you, the late Gary Provost, for expressing in a single sentence how we relate our own life to a shape that repeats in a common storyline of drama and value. What we do to others we do to ourselves. Thank you, all who confidently fine-tuned the end product. I am grateful to the late Charlotte Lewis, who made my dream pictures come true. Joan Pinkert and many others thoughtfully organized a body of information.

This is how my book grew; this is how I grow. To make the tree whole, we have to know where the branches are broken. Creativity and courage strengthen the broken places of each tree growing from root to branches.

love and laughter,

Trudy

"*We learn to like ourselves for
who we really are—a truly original,
never-before, never-again living person.
Only one of you in a timeless web of cells.*"

Ardys Reverman

Foreword

Over the ages, artists of all types have tried everything to touch the human soul. When they succeed — when the painting is treasured or reproduced for others, when the story is retold again and again, when the song is sung a thousand times — we say the art has worked.

When we look at the entire body of art that has worked we can ask ourselves: What is true of most of the songs that worked? Most of the paintings? Most of the stories? The answer to that question is craft. Craft is that part of art that can be predicted, taught, and repeated.

My own field, of course, is storytelling and storytelling has its craft. It is called structure. But story structure is not something that writers invented: It is something that we observe. We observe that there are certain aspects of story that resonate with the human tuning fork, just as there are clumsy efforts at story that, lacking harmony, are thrown away. Readers like happy endings, not unhappy endings. They like to see a man or woman succeed through their own efforts, not luck or coincidence. They like big stakes, balanced conflict, clear goals, personal growth, a meaningful and noble struggle, a very dark moment before the light, and the victory of good over evil. Take away any one of these elements, and the reader feels that something is missing.

If anyone wonders whether people everywhere are the same, I suggest he listen to their stories. From century to century, from hemisphere to hemisphere, the same story structure satisfies, delights, enlightens, and inspires readers. It is not because people have been taught to like the same stories. It is because story structure is dictated by human nature. The mind of the reader is an essential chemical in the formula of the story. You cannot separate the reader from the story anymore than you can separate the water from the wave. Ask a hundred children to draw Jack and his beanstalks and they will all draw it differently.

And they will all draw it correctly.

—*Gary Provost*

(The late Gary Provost was the author of *Make Your Words Work*, and with his wife Gail, he is the author of *Good If It Goes*, winner of the National Jewish Book Award for Children's Literature.)

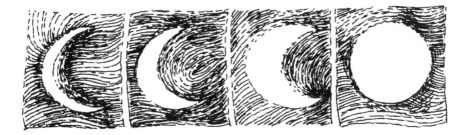

Preface

This is a book meant to be shared and talked about together. Many parts have activities and questions. They can be done alone or answered quietly internally. But most are intended as the beginning of a discussion between child and adult. The overall purpose is understanding — of ourselves and of others. And conversation is a wonderful path to greater understanding.

To help each of us to better recognize his or her place in the scheme of things, I am reintroducing four animal icons, the Synergy Pals, each displaying different senses and values, each having a different personality. They were first seen in the book *heart2heart: Be Yourself — Everyone Else Is Taken*. (See also www.synergypals.com for more information about these four helpers.) Lookabout Lion is a visionary, demanding freedom to turn the system around. Talkabout Chimp is a mover and shaker who afflicts the comfortable with radical ideas for understanding. Thinkabout Owl is the spotter of order, detailing the forest as well as the trees. Feelabout Koala is the static cling of emotions, vibrating with pain or pleasure, longing for harmony. Working together, they learn that teamwork is child's play and synergy is nature's way of redirecting uninvited chaos.

Inborn, dynamic values drive our behavior. But we must constantly deal with people who think and do differently than us — and do so successfully — if we are to have growing relationships that last and teams that work in which our unique gifts come together. An explorer, a detailer, a planner, and a nurturer make a good fit working together and create a synergistic force that frees them to find more meaningful relationships. We want to bring up our children with the knowledge of the differing gifts inside them and the ways to keep those gifts in balance with their outer environments, especially other people.

We need each other, no matter how different we all are. Inability to appreciate others' values throws life out of balance. Understanding others' unique ways of doing and seeing gives us a framework in which we can turn disorders into skills (not pills) and make harmful choices less likely. Perhaps our hardest mission is to provide a safe responsive environment in which children can question and be heard. Looking at our natural talents as adaptive traits helps us to learn how to be each other's best teachers.

Like Rip Van Winkle, we've been asleep, but as we wake to new possibilities, we need to put our adaptive traits to work. By embracing teams, we can use our diverse skills and increased energy to bring about a global change of mind and heart, transforming our human story. Great social transformations move below the surface of turbulent events, finding form gradually. As we struggle together toward new paradigms, the synergy of order, freedom, understanding, and harmony can bring us to a common sense of love and hope. Join my Synergy Pals in appreciating the wonderful differences in children: the complementary talents that create all human accomplishment in discovering what's right with the world.

love and laughter,

Judy

Contents

*We come spinning out of nothingness,
scattering stars like dust.*

—*Rumi*
1207 – 1273

Research validates why opposites attract or why I fell in love with your brain.

Highly creative people tend to grow up in families that respect and embody opposites. Adults encourage uniqueness, yet provide stability. They are highly responsive to childrens' needs, yet challenge children to develop skills and adaptability. Developmental theories state that the mind has four levels corresponding to four different sets of skills.

 The first to develop are gross motor skills (**SF-Sensing Feeling**) **Feel**about Koala which develop during the first year of childhood. These involve rhythm and control.

 Next to develop are fine motor skills (**ST-Sensing Thinking**) **Think**about Owl which involve positioning and dexterity, and develop between the ages of one and two.

 Third to develop are verbal skills (**NF-N-Intuition Feeling**) **Talk**about Chimp which involve intonation and words, and which originate around the age of two.

 Last to develop are intellectual skills (**NT-N-Intuition Thinking**) **Look**about Lion which develop sometime after the age of eight and which involve planning and conclusion.

One area of typological analysis of particular interest is learning type or styles. There is a surprising convergence in this area of the senses (think, look, talk and feel) to Carl Jung's four basic perceiving and judging functions.

Introduction

The Synergy Pals®

Out beyond ideas of wrongdoing and rightdoing,
there is a field. I'll meet you there.

—Rumi
1207 – 1273

The Friendly Universe Discovery Exploration Certificate

Teammates give their best to all the rest
with each as part of the whole.
This certifies that:

_____

- ❤ Investigated facts, obtained results, experienced hands-on activities, and developed new ideas.

- ❤ Journeyed to inner space and explored the galaxy of Natural Talents on the Starship Self propelled by Synergy Drive.

- ❤ Found the Friendly Universe full of Order, Freedom, Understanding, and Harmony in a dynamic synergy system.

- ❤ After a close encounter of a personal kind, discovered the local life form is friendly, polite, smart, and funny.

- ❤ Is encouraged to plan further explorations because the Friendly Universe goes on and is subject to change.

You are hereby awarded the honor of Exploration Captain of the Friendly Universe, First Class

This _____ day of _____, 20___

Dr. Ardy and the Synergy Pals

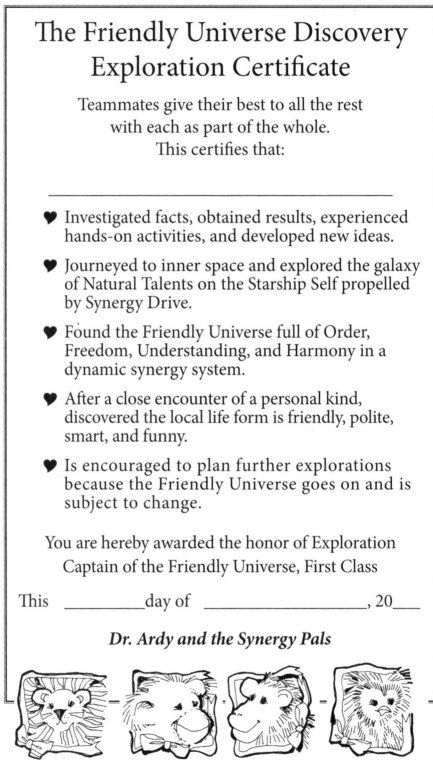

Talkabout Chimp—The Dream Mover

I am someone who likes to share ideas, talk, listen, and have hunches in bunches.

Through my Talkabout window, I share inspired ideas, directing others to understand and be understood.

I am a Talkabout Chimp who likes to listen and talk about ideas and have understanding. I like to run my own show and take safe risks. I am more effective if I focus and organize my energy.

Talkabout Chimp's natural talents move us toward understanding, ideas, and creativity.

I love curiosity and questions about ideas and dreams that show people how to be people. I say, "Let me tell you about this fantastic new idea. Tell me what you think of it."

Others appreciate their ideas:

☼ Let's play with it and see what happens if we do it differently.

☼ Given what we know is true, it's possible that…

☼ Let's find out what's on the other side of that mountain.

Thinkabout Owl—The Skill Master

I am someone who likes to sit in my room where I feel safe as I quietly think and work by myself. I like to carefully figure things out and put everything in order, with new systems becoming new habits.

Through my Thinkabout window, I know how to gather details, make plans and to keep order and safety.

I am a Thinkabout Owl, who likes to be safe at home, having things in order and time to think, contemplating perfection. To grow, I accept unknowns.

Thinkabout Owl's natural talents move us toward order, facts, and safety.

It's okay for me to like details, to want things in order, and to see patterns in all things. I say, "Once we get all the facts in order, we'll know the best way to do things."

Others appreciate their accuracy in specific tasks well done:

☼ Here's what we already know.

☼ I can see how the information fits into this project.

☼ Take a model—if it isn't broken, how can we make it better?

☼ I've been thinking; we know enough about it to try something new.

Lookabout Lion—The Vision Leader

I am someone who likes to have choices and make quick decisions. I am able to work out a plan in my mind and get results in any project that I choose.

Through my Lookabout window, I see a world to explore and feel I have the freedom to take charge.

I am a Lookabout Lion who likes to get results, have a zillion choices, and be a free spirit. To grow, I accept limits.

**Lookabout Lion's natural talents
move us towards freedom, choice, and results.**

I feel good when everyone cooperates. I take charge to make sure the job is done well, to show people how to live better. I say, "We'll get somewhere only if we choose what we want to have happen."

Others appreciate their ingenuity and curiosity:

☼ I've looked at the problem completely and carefully.

☼ Here's a picture to show you where we are.

☼ Let's make a model to see if the material will work.

☼ I understand what we're trying to do.

☼ There may be more than one way to do it.

Feelabout Koala—The Peacekeeper

I am someone who loves to make and touch things. When I know everyone around me is friendly, I like to share my feelings and talk.

Through my Feelabout window, I feel how to create harmony, especially how to help friends get along with each other.

I am a Feelabout Koala who likes to touch things, feel at peace with the world, and be with my friends. I act to create goodwill. To grow, I face uncertainty and set goals.

Feelabout Koala's natural talents move us towards harmony, belonging, and hands-on skills.

I love parties and celebrations where I can listen to the gentle laughter of my friends while we all eat, link, and be merry. I say, "I made it just for you; I knew you'd like it."

Others appreciate their easygoing nature:

☼ You have to handle things with just the force they need, not more or less.

☼ It's okay the way it is, but let's move a few things around a little.

☼ This won't hurt it.

☼ We can build it together if we all lend a hand.

When I Am Part of the Whole.

The Thinkabout Owl, Lookabout Lion,
Talkabout Chimp, and Feelabout Koala
Learn how to stay healthy and have fun
Through all the work and play,
One and all, every day.
Each is part of the whole.

The Lion, Chimp, Koala, and Owl
All name their troubles and tell themselves,
"Now I'll learn from the rest and be my best
When I am part of the whole."

The Chimp, Koala, Owl, and Lion
Learn a lot when they try on
One another's feelings.
It really is healing
Seeing each as part of the whole.

The Koala, Owl, Lion, and Chimp
All learn how to be loving,
And to make it simple.
Yet they each give their best to all the rest
When each is part of the whole.

Mother Earth and her children belong together;
all are connected, working as one, to discover
in a spirit of wonder how to bring about
the best for the future.

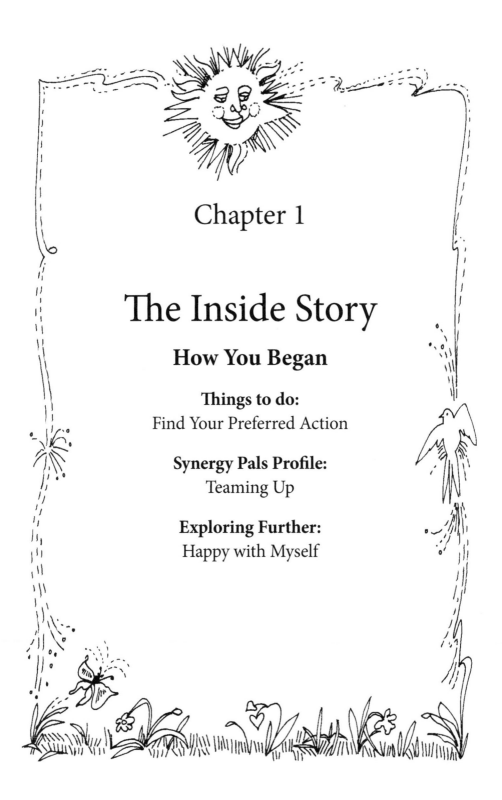

Chapter 1

The Inside Story

How You Began

Things to do:
Find Your Preferred Action

Synergy Pals Profile:
Teaming Up

Exploring Further:
Happy with Myself

How You Began

Once upon a time...

when you and I were born,
love's earthly miracle unfolded
in tiny baby bodies.
We soon discovered that
what's inside matters most.

There is a promise in all of us,
to become the best we can be.

Each of us is like a seed ready to grow.
Already rooted in some part of our nature
is the stuff of the spirit, just as inborn as the
body, mind, and all of our senses.

We each find something to stand for and enjoy in our miracle of life. Little steps move us forward each day. Searching far and wide we get to know our very own style.

How can we help each other? If we understand that we share common needs, we can give our hearts to one another. We create a world of belonging as fully as we can.

In the beginning, we are bound to nature with our very first breaths, feeling nature's rhythm in our mother's soothing heartbeat lullaby. This is why we feel a longing for balance with all living creatures. Mother Earth and her children belong together; all are connected, working as one, to discover in a spirit of wonder how to bring about the best for the future.

Each of us is an original, wanting to express something of our very own. We have language so we can put our feelings into words, but words can unite or divide us. We speak the same word language as the people around us, yet, we may miss the meaning of what is said, the heart of what matters most. When that happens, we go right past one another, without understanding the feelings in each other's hearts.

You learn to think about things in different ways. Pleasure marks the way you feel and behave when you expect the best. Sadness marks the way you feel or behave when you expect the worst.

Feelings are something important that we can't see and sometimes can't figure out. Certain ones may be real and true for our selves but not for others. We all share the deeply rooted values of understanding, order, freedom, and harmony, but one of these may be more important to you than to me.

With our first newborn cry we begin asking: What do I think, and why do I feel a certain way? Where do I come from? Where do I want to go? Do you care about me? Can I learn to work with you rather than trying to change you? How do we make it comfortable to live and work with each other?

When we first find our own voice, we begin to listen more to ourselves than to other people. Other people's ideas of who we should be and how we should act may make us feel unhappy.

And we may start to notice that each of us has two parts: the Outside and the Inside. Only one of you in a timeless web of cells.

The Outside is the body, an Earth suit of our own. Each of us has a wonderfully different Outside — to suit the way each most likes to do things.

And the inside? Still cradled deep in our memory, we hear our heart's rhythm connecting us through time. We discover we see things as we are, not as they are. Don't believe everything you are thinking.

The Dance of Life

Partnership is an adventure into who you are and what you care about. The tensions of our opposites attract us to become each other's best teachers.

Even when we can't hear a voice, we trust what we feel. Inside is where our feelings and thoughts live. It's where we get excited about what we want to do and focus on what gifts we are here to give back.

Our lives bend and bow, connecting us to some things more than others. We move into action and discover our talents.

Be yourself from the inside out in harmony, because everybody else is already taken. Knowing what we want to become helps make it easy to give others what they want. We give and take with those who matter most in our lives.

We can understand what we value by feeling what matters to us most. Our deepest concerns tell us about a purpose bigger than ourselves. When we know what is important to us, we can think about what is important to others.

We learn to like ourselves for who we really are — a truly original, never-before, never-again living person.

What has to happen to become truly you?

Our common senses show us things as they change energies. Just watch as the seasons change from Fall to Winter to Spring to Summer. Living on purpose in the endless cycle of life is a natural process for change. Working together, our differences make a good fit, connecting our gifts to a common purpose.

Wiggle your body, take your shoes off, walk on the grass, put your back to a grand old tree. The tree's roots nourish new life, building on the past, and growing into the new day.

Sending out leaves to the sun, its edges stretch into the unknown. We come from the roots of our grandma and grandpa tree, trees to love and be loved for ourselves.

Things to Do: Find Your Preferred Action

For each subject in the chart below, find the action that best suits you. For example, if you were in a play, how would you like to help? In each row, circle your first choice.

Action Chart			
	Thinkabout	**Lookabout**	**Talkabout**	**Feelabout**
A play	Edit	Direct	Perform	Cheer
A kite	Test	Design	Fly	Build
Your room	Organize	Plan	Transform	Personalize
How to help	Give facts	Ask experts	Start ideas	Cooperate
A report	Research	Write	Present	Critique
Promptness	Arrive on time	Want others to be on time	Usually on time	Sometimes on time
Ways to learn	Practice	Experience	Discover	Imitate

You'll likely find that what you prefer to do for all activities falls under one of the four columns. And each of your friends probably has a preferred column, but it may not match yours. Choose something to do that uses the combined talents of your group of friends. (Make sure each of the four actions for your chosen activity is the preferred one for one of you.) You need to cover all of them to get the job done well.

Remember to let others do the jobs they like. A whole activity needs all members. Teams use thinking as a tool. It is important for your team to play together. Why is it important to work together to accomplish tasks? Because:

♥ Listening to the ideas from clever Talkabout friends' inner voices helps them focus and finish tasks.

♥ Checking in from time to time with organized Thinkabout friends gets them into the fun.

♥ Being kind to our brave Lookabout friends helps them understand us.

♥ And helping friendly Feelabout friends guides us all in time training.

Synergy Pals Profile: Teaming Up

Thinkabout Skill Master:
Thinks about the right way.

Lookabout Vision Leader:
Looks about for a new way.

Feelabout Peace Maker:
Feels about for an easier way.

Talkabout Dream Mover:
Talks about the fun way.

When you and your Synergy Pals team up to work together, you use your strengths, weaknesses, and differences to get jobs done and have fun. When we see how the parts work together, we can do so much more — help others, lead others, encourage others, and inspire others.

Exploring Further: Happy With Myself

Remember When: See how you feel about the statements below. Which are most like you? Which are not like you? Could you choose differently? What is important to you? What is important to your friends or your parents? Ask your friends or parents about their choices.

I feel happy with myself when I am . . .

…helping my friends get along together and being thanked for my help. *Harmony* and action are most important.

…putting my belongings in order so I can find things when I need them. *Order* and service are most important.

…sharing my ideas to get others excited about solving problems. *Understanding* and making changes are most important.

…picturing a plan and explaining how to get it done quickly and correctly. *Freedom* and knowledge are most important.

Talk about your values with a parent or teacher: *order*, *harmony*, *freedom*, and *understanding*. Talk about how we each like the different responses (above). How do we teach and change each other?

Talk about the difference between what you do and what you think. What do you feel you do best?

You will discover one activity that may seem easy for you and some activities may be hard for you. You might notice how you are alike and different from your friends! What type are you?

Just My Style

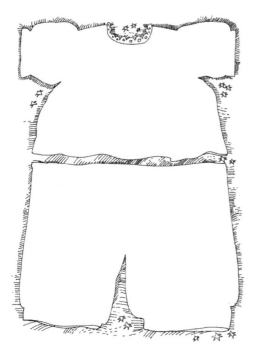

Do you have a favorite color? What colors do you like to wear? Bright? Light? Dark? Calm colors? Warm colors? Or Cool?

Which do you like best? Spring, Summer, Fall, or Winter clothes? How do you feel when you wear your favorite clothes? What is it about them that makes them your favorite? Are they loose? Tight? Soft? Smooth? Is it the way they fit? The way they look? What they're made of? Or the way they make you feel?

When you think about the way you look, sound, and move, what do you like best about YOU?

How do you like to move? Some people are very still, others move all of the time, like a rocking chair in motion.

What shape is your body?

Round? Small? Tall? Slim? Husky?

What color is your skin?

If you were ice cream, What flavor would you be?

What color are your eyes?

Like brown earth? The blue sky? The green sea? Or like some flowers or leaves?

What is your hair like?

Long? Short? Light? Dark? Straight? Curly?

Just as the earth rotates around the sun, and the moon circles around the earth, our thoughts, feelings, and actions have a certain spin quality to them as well.

Look for the idea of "spin" in the language we use:

"I have this idea that's been going 'round and 'round in my head."

"I keep talking in circles about this problem."

"Let's put a new spin on that idea."

"I keep looping around on what I should do next."

"I'm all wound up."

"I keep spinning this idea in my head."

"I need to go unwind."

Chapter 2

The Outside Story

How You Look and Sound

Things to Do:
Differences

Synergy Pal's Profile:
My Preferences

Exploring Further:
Play

How You Look and Sound

What's in a Name?

Ella Ella Bo Bella,

Anna Banana Bom Bella

Mie My Mo Mella

OH Ella

Our names are very special! We are given names almost as soon as we are born. Do you know how or why your name was chosen for you?

To choose a name to give their baby, some parents look through big books full of names. These books also tell the meaning of each name. Does your name have a meaning? Is it the name of someone else in your family history? Were you named after someone your parents admired?

Maybe your parents were imaginative and gave you an especially different name. Maybe they just liked the sound of your name.

How do you feel about your whole name when it is written? Do you like the way it looks? Do people call you by a name that is not your real name?

Caroline · Alex · Liza · Kristin · Peter · Jack · Oliver · Orlando · Pierre · Ursula

How do you feel about your name when you say it to others? When others say it to you? Do you like the sound of your name? Would you change your name if you could? Write your name and its meaning on this line.

_____

For a moment, pretend that you did choose your own real name. Does your name tell you something about who you are, how you want to live your life, or what you want to learn from your life?

Why would you choose your own name for yourself? When you think about your name, what good things about yourself come to mind?

Look up the meaning of your name and tell a story to someone about why that meaning is important to you. Patterns are revealed in names.

Write your autograph and ask your friends to write their autographs in this frame.

Your desire to "be and feel you" is very important.

Star Qualities

Our bodies and minds are made of original stardust, the same stuff that's in everything from the largest star to the tiniest sea creature and everything in between -- including you and me. Happy molecules are a bubble bath for the mind.

We are all made of the same elements. Waves and particles of light are made with care for us, as we think and create. Each of us is put together in a new and different way. Each of us has a special pattern that tells others who we are.

Your body looks like you so people can recognize you. When people say your name, they remember how your body looks and moves. And when people see your body they remember your name, face, voice, and how they feel about you. (Well, almost always.)

Sometimes people can recognize you at a distance even when they can't see your face. Because they know how you move, they know it's you. Do your eyes light up when your friend walks into the room?

What favorite things do you like to wear? How do you imagine you look to others? Do you like to do what others do, as well as have your own say, to be something of your very own?

Draw a portrait of yourself wearing your favorite clothes. Add as many details as you like.

How do you feel when you play dress-up, taking delight in the world of make-believe and memories? Pretending to be someone else can be fun. But remember that whatever you wear on the outside, you are always the same you on the inside. That's your core that is always with you.

To Wander and Wonder

To be myself, I need to learn to seek out new ideas, know my strong and weak points, keep my future focused, practice my skills, belong when I am with others, and know my own and others' limits. The challenge is to grow, move, and work together. Remember—energy flows where attention goes.

By following your heart, you find your values. Intend it!

ORDER

FREEDOM

HARMONY

UNDERSTANDING

Things to Do: Differences

Talk with your team about how the Synergy Pals' differences might cause problems. Looking at each Pal's square on page 39, who seems more like you today? Did you feel like a different Pal yesterday? Could you feel like another Pal tomorrow? Why do we like different things at different times? Good teamwork gives us a better way to see different points of view in ourselves and others.

How do our core values fit together? Play a role in each square, putting yourself in each Pal's place to see a different point of view.

Write or tell a story about one of these three ideas:

♥ All four types are in each of us and we know how we fit well with others.

♥ Learning to cooperate with the four different personality types around us will change our lives.

♥ No one knows what is best or has all of the answers. The world is always changing.

Synergy Pals Profile: My Preferences

Do you prefer watching or telling? Make solid the part of the dotted line that describes you—prefers watching or prefers telling. Now do the same for the line for prefers thinking or prefers feeling. Your two lines mark two sides of one of the four boxes. Do the statements inside your box match with how you see yourself?

Outline your preferred inner square using the following colors: Owl/green, Lion/blue, Chimp/yellow, Koala/red.

think—direct

prefers thinking

Order
Facts
Safety
Finishes work
Prefers calm colors
Neat/neat
Thinks things over
Takes time making decisions
Answers questions when asked
Listens to and watches others

Freedom
Choices
Results
Seeks knowledge
Prefers cool colors
Neat/messy
Implements plans
Makes decisions quickly
Answers questions and talks
Tells others what to do

watch—direct

tell—direct

— *prefers watching* — + — · *prefers telling* —

prefers feeling

Harmony
Belonging
Activity
Starts action
Prefers warm colors
Messy/neat
Feels things intuitively
Takes time making decisions
Asks questions and listens
Asks others

Understanding
Ideas
Creativity
Inspires ideas
Prefers bright colors
Messy/messy
Takes risks
Makes decisions quickly
Answers questions and talks
Creates new ideas

feel—indirect

Exploring Further: Play

Discuss how you feel about the multiple-choice answers to the unfinished statement below. Which do you like most? Least? Why? Discuss how and why we each choose a different response.

I like to play games that . . .
   … everyone can play and have fun playing, and no one loses (heart2heart, playing ball or dancing).
   … have rules, a lot of action, and a winner (card games or football).
   … make me think or plan ahead (checkers and Monopoly).
   … let me use my imagination (Pictionary or charades).

New ways of seeing, talking, feeling, and thinking create a whole new world for us. We talk about things we believe in to discover what we really want and need and how we'll feel when we get it. Two people do not need the same beliefs to have a good friendship. With awareness of dynamic differences we are less likely to make choices that hurt each other.

The same goes for our play values. We may feel bad when the fun goes out of something we do. And when we feel bad, we may act in a bad way—by lying, cheating, stealing, bullying, gossiping, blaming or running away.

To change the way you feel, focus on what you like about you! Picture a time of your own success. What do you see? What do you say to yourself? What turns your good feelings on? Take action! Efforts you are proud of make you happy, a force for good.

Live life as happily you can with family and friends. Life is a gift to help each other develop.

Happy molecules are
a bubble bath for the mind.

Every thought of yours is a real thing—a force.
Prentice Milford 1834-1891

Chapter 3

Mind Map at a Glance

A Picture of Your Thoughts

Things to Do:
Discover Your Core Values

Synergy Pals Profile:
Values

Exploring Further:
Important Values

A Picture of Your Thoughts

Every day we learn new things and form ideas about our discoveries — in school, at home, from friends, parents, teachers, and others. We use our senses as we change our minds and feelings about things.

These ideas make up a sort of landscape that circles, builds, collides, crosses over, and slides into place in our minds. Just as a normal map shows relationships between physical things around us, this inner map represents the relationships between the ideas and beliefs we understand. We put our discoveries on an "inner map" in our mind. The inner map changes when we add to or change our beliefs. The mind hops around and puts new ways of seeing things onto our maps. For example you know how to set goals by "keeping your eye on the ball even when you can't see the ball," or perhaps you may focus by saying, "I'm getting my head together." These ideas are places on your inner map.

We see, hear, touch, taste, and smell the world and write new things on our inner maps.

Some of us like picture maps, to draw in our minds the things we see through our eyes.

Some of us make maps of sounds we hear in our minds
— the music of words and tones we hear with our ears.

Some of us have maps of feeling, movement, and the action, impressions, and emotions that run through our bodies.

Some of us have step-by-step maps of detailed information that we sort out and make sense of through our thoughts.

Maps and Beliefs

Most of us don't know much about our inner maps, yet they contain a lot of information about our needs and beliefs about the world. Pay attention to your inner map to understand what's happening in your mind.

Each of us has different abilities and might think and feel differently about the same experience. Let your senses lead the way. Which of the four styles of inner map do you like?

Seeing? Talking? Feeling? Thinking?

Most people don't just use one style. All of the styles are available for each of us to use doing well and doing good.

How does our inner map of pictures, words, facts, and movement tell us what we believe is happening in our world?

We each favor two or more senses. Nobody is eager to use a style that is difficult, and yet we grow by learning to appreciate other ways of seeing and doing things. Learning to work with differences is the way we learn to adapt.

What sensations are you seeing, hearing, tasting, smelling, or touching as you recall a happy thought? How about when you make useful choices? How are you showing outside what satisfaction you are experiencing inside?

Mapping Good Feelings

When we focus on how we think and behave, we understand more about our feelings. We all win if we learn something from what we do. We learn to make a good fit with others. We learn that we proudly accomplish things.

Think of a time when you felt good. Put the feeling with a movement, like clapping or waving or thumbs-up, and say "Yes!" out loud. You can make yourself pay attention to your good feelings!

Talking to yourself while you make a happy movement is a new habit that can make you feel good while doing something difficult. Try saying "I want to…" instead of "I have to…." See if it makes you happier with what you're doing. Feeling positive is the best way to use your skills and talents every day on every step of your life journey.

Below are some purposeful activities or ways of being that people feel are important. Rank each of the ten items from 1, for what is most important to you, to 10 for least important.

___ receiving praise   ___ being safe

___ achieving something   ___ being independent

___ owning things   ___ creating things

___ belonging to a group   ___ being successful

___ being self-confident   ___ helping others

Things to Do: Discover Your Core Values

We have many other values we believe are important besides understanding, order, freedom, and harmony. Perhaps you can recognize some of them. On the list of values, circle the one of each pair that is more important to you.

Synergy Pals Profile: Values
What do you value the most now?

To find out, circle only one of each pair on each line:

Achieving something	or	Feeling safe
Having things	or	Helping others
Belonging to a group	or	Receiving praise
Being independent	or	Being successful
Being creative	or	Belonging to a group
Being successful	or	Feeling safe
Being self-confident	or	Being creative
Receiving praise	or	Achieving something
Feeling safe	or	Having things
Helping others	or	Belonging to a group
Being successful	or	Helping others
Having things	or	Being creative
Feeling safe	or	Receiving praise
Being independent	or	Being self-confident
Being creative	or	Being successful
Achieving something	or	Being creative
Being self-confident	or	Belonging to a group
Receiving praise	or	Being independent
Belonging to a group	or	Having things
Helping others	or	Achieving something

Count the number of times you circled each of the following ten values. Put that number on the line in front of each. Which ones did you circle 4 times? Those are your strongest values. Mark them with a special symbol, maybe a star. Do they match with how you think of yourself?

___ Achieving something

___ Having things

___ Belong to a group

___ Being independent

___ Being creative

___ Being successful

___ Being self-confident

___ Receiving praise

___ Feeling safe

___ Helping others

Interests expand like the growth rings of a tree, with more and more added as you get older. Knowing what is important to you and how to get it is the key to growth. Your values and interests reflect your inner wants — your map — and will not always be the same.

Whenever you get what you want, you'll find that you want something else. It's always something, because motivations work to feed the brain. Think about what you want, think about how good it would feel to have it, and link "feel good" thoughts to it. Doing this for yourself is your growing edge, like those of the branches and roots of a tree.

There's always a way. Love needs to motivate us to tap into universal values and behavior. Do whatever it takes to get your feet moving towards your goals.

Feeling bored limits us. Feeling comfortable all of the time limits us. Sometimes we are afraid to try something different because it might be uncomfortable. Decide to outgrow your fears by taking action. Mark Twain said, "If you have to eat a frog, do it first thing in the morning." He meant that we should do that unfamiliar thing right away, and not spend the day becoming more and more afraid of doing it.

When you search for what you like to do best, you can also learn more about other people. When we know more about others, we work well with them and get more done than we could by ourselves. The steps you take—your journey—are more important than the goal, because the journey shows you what matters most in your life.

Ask yourself what is the most important thing to you now. What would you like to have happen to get the results you want? What three steps do you have to take now to reach that goal? What can you do each day to make sure you accomplish what you truly want.

What you choose to give as gifts also shows what you value. And it tells how you would like to be thanked. Write or tell a story or perform a dance that shares how you would thank others for the part they played on a team.

Thinkabout Owl remembers jobs well done with traditional flowers, presents, and a card. Feelabout Koala gives a last-minute surprise party with a personal touch. Talkabout Chimp tells a meaningful story. Lookabout Lion gives elegant gifts, and rewards tasks well done.

Exploring Further: Important Values

Look at the numbers you wrote under Synergy Pals Profile: Values on page 53. Below put an "X" in front of the values that are your strongest from that exercise. Talk with friends about how your values motivate each of you differently.

It is important for me. . .

☐ **achieving something,** and it makes me feel proud. For some of us, it's very important to be proud of what we're doing and that others like what we're doing.

☐ **having things** (clothes or games) I like, or that I can earn the money to buy it. For some of us, it's important to own things or earn the money we spend.

☐ **belonging to a group**—that others accept me, that I feel I belong to a team. Sometimes approval of others is important to us. We need to feel accepted as someone others enjoy and want to be with.

☐ **being independent.** I'm free to choose what I do. Some of us need to know we're in charge of what we do.

☐ **being creative,** doing new things, and having people come to me for ideas. Some of us enjoy being able to think of new ways to do things.

☐ **being successful.** People want me to be good at what I like to do. Sometimes, what pleases us most is feeling that our goals are being reached, our skills are being recognized, and work we've done is getting results.

☐ **being self-confident**. People listen to what I have to say. Some of us need to feel that others listen and treat our ideas with respect. If we want others to help us with something we think is important, they will.

☐ **being praised**. People who matter to me notice me. Some of us need to hear words of approval for what we do well.

☐ **feeling safe**. I want to know what tomorrow will bring. For some of us, having a safe home and no fears about the future matter most in life.

☐ **helping others** in order to be in harmony. I bring my friends together. For some of us, helping others is what makes us feel worthwhile and useful.

After exploring these values you might talk with your friends about how your most important value motivates your own inner map. Also ask them what is important to them. Draw, color, doodle in this book to make it valuable to you.

At this moment
someone is thinking good thoughts of you!

Chapter 4

Starting Point

Life Is a Journey

Things to do:
Nature Walk

Synergy Pals Profile:
When I Feel Threatened

Exploring Further:
Reflect

Life Is a Journey

Only YOU can make your journey of self-discovery into the story that's all about YOU.

Every year, on the same day, each of us marks the beginning of another year of life on earth. This day, of course, is your BIRTHDAY!

It's the very first event of our lives. Though nearly everything else in our lives may change, our birthday stays the same. What do you like best about your birthday? Is there anything you would change? When is your birthday? In what season of the year?

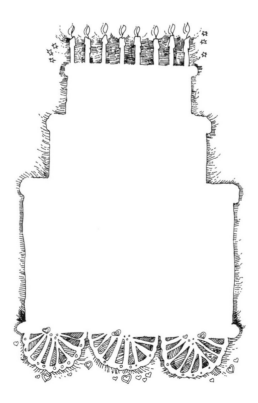

Draw and color the biggest birthday feeling you remember, like the Fourth of July in the USA. How will it be reborn with memories every year?

How is nature showing us birthdays all year round with predictable patterns when events occur. Think how nature arranges the seasons by changing colors and temperatures and length of days.

Think of the sounds of each season: rustling leaves, pouring rain, crunching ice, howling wind, singing birds, buzzing insects.

Can you come up with other colors, sounds, tastes, smells, and feelings that make the seasons your own?

Were you born in the SPRING when yellow dandelions bloom to greet you and bare-branched trees grow tiny leaves like the creation of tiny new ideas?

 Were you born in the SUMMER when the sun is hot in the clear, blue sky and children play freely about under shady trees?

Were you born in the FALL when the nights are crisp and cool and children jump in piles of red, crunchy leaves fallen from the trees?

 Were you born in the WINTER when it is cold and clear and perfect snowflakes fall, making the ground all white and the green fir trees twinkle with frost?

Nature expresses herself with different seasons, different colors, different moods, turning the calendar wheel of the year.

Although our Outside may be born in a certain season, our Inside is more like nature, because we express ourselves in different ways at different times.

Gather in a group and pretend you are the different seasons, playing music, dancing, and play-acting in different colors and moods.

Imagine what you'd feel and think, what you'd hear, see, smell, and touch in each season as the energy moves. Share your stories, dances, and pictures with each other.

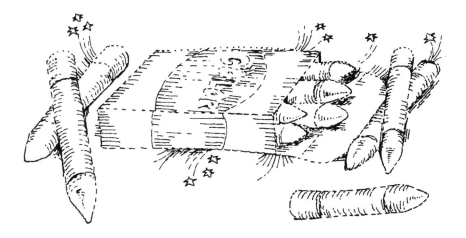

What do I like to imagine in SPRING when the days are
all new and fresh, light and yellow, and bright ideas
are filling my head?

What do I like to do most in SUMMER when days are sunny and I'm playing outside under the big, blue sky, feeling everything is possible?

How do I like to feel in FALL when days feel friendly
and cozy, when red leaves are tumbling down, when I'm
laughing and playing with my friends?

What do I like to think about in WINTER when days are quiet and peaceful, calm like tall green fir trees, while I'm putting my thoughts in order?

Which of the seasons is most like you?

It's hard to choose a season if you only look at the Outside of yourself because you're more than that. What's inside you is a bigger part of who you are and connects you to one of the seasons.

It's easy to see Inside ourselves when we look with our hearts. A heart that really wants to know gives us enough light to see how we really feel. It's just like looking through a window to see who's at home INSIDE.

It's good to know all about who lives Inside of YOU. When you understand more about yourself Inside and what comes naturally to your heart, you'll find it easier to understand all about yourself.

Things to Do: Nature Walk

To feel an inner closeness to nature, take a walk outdoors away from busy streets! Notice what attracts you in nature. Is it the sounds — wind blowing through the leaves? The smells — strong scents of summer blossoms? The sights — brilliant display of autumn's trees? Seasons reveal a beautiful circle of color as they change from light to dark, lush to bare, and move from winter's rest to awakening spring, playful summer, fall harvest.

Look at a color wheel to discover different moods, tones, texture, hues. Brainstorm ideas, linking nature to each type of thinking and feeling.

Make up your own colorful nature rhymes.

Sunny Yellow inspires ideas so bold
Laughing out loud or discovering gold.

Pine needle path leads steadily Green
Footprints show where we've been.

Deep Blue sky and foam-tossed sea
Picture future successes for me.

Rosy Red shimmering sunrise
tugs my heart with daily surprise.

Synergy Pals Profile: When I Feel Threatened

Thinkabout Owl

When threatened I may act . . .
Stony
Picky
Deliberate
Bored
Stubborn
Suspicious
. . . because I feel bad.

I need to learn how to . . .
Express my feelings
Be spontaneous
Just get started
Enjoy unstructured time
Get along with active people
Trust other's decisions
. . . to feel good.

Feelabout Koala

When threatened I may act . . .
Lonely
Afraid
Gullible
Sneaky
Guilty
Careless
Impulsive
. . . because I feel bad.

I need to learn how to . . .
Be independent
Be honest about feelings
Be assertive and set goals
Be confident
Follow through
Know my boundaries
. . . to feel good.

I Need to Learn How to

Lookabout Lion

When threatened I may act . . .
Bossy
Blunt
Unfeeling
Serious
Demanding
Like I "know it all"
. . . because I feel bad.

I need to learn how to . . .
Not be so demanding
Consider other's needs
Listen to feelings
Laugh and be more fun
Relax and slow down
Poke fun at myself
. . . to feel good.

Talkabout Chimp

When threatened I may act . . .
Scattered
Let down
Overwhelmed
Pushy
Naïve
Worried
. . . because I feel bad.

I need to learn how to . . .
Organize details
Follow through
Plan ahead
Listen to others
Be practical
Delegate jobs
. . . to feel good.

Exploring Further: Reflect

Imagine a very great tree, as old as time itself.

This grand tree grows just as you do. The strong trunk lifts up its branching arms, unfolding new leaves to the sun. The sun feeds the leaves as they grow until it is time for them to change color and fall to earth.

Moss softens the earth around the trunk, and four huge roots drink, far below the leaves and branches. Relax and take a deep breath, listening to the tree's soft sounds with creatures overhead and underfoot in nature's song of oneness. Close your eyes and taste the air — smell the perfumes of growing things all around the tree.

Imagine that the growth rings of the tree are singing a secret song for you. Your heart is happy and whole, and you feel you have a place in this time. Like the growth rings of the tree, you grow from the core of your heart, with many roots, forming your whole being. Deep in our hearts, we all want to give to others, to grow, to do something important in the world. We share the need to find our heart-gifts.

Like a tree, your growing edge gets stronger, your branches stretch out, and your great trunk and roots support you. The Heartwood Tree within you grows tall, reaching for the light of understanding.

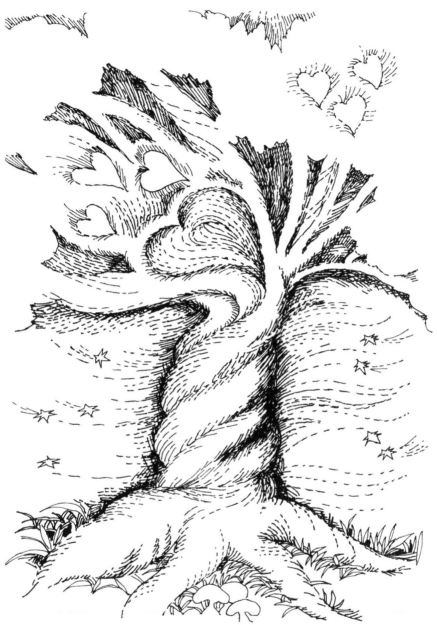

*The trees in the street are old trees used to living
with people, family trees that remember your
grandfather's name.*
—A child

Doodle or write new things to your inner map here.

Chapter 5

Hand-me Down Genes

Where Ideas Come From

Things to do:
Find a Hero

Synergy Pals Profile:
Understanding Each Other

Exploring Further:
Work Styles

Where Ideas Come From

We are born with a map of jumping genes, cells from our parents mixing around to become us.

That map has all of our information in our genes — some parts of our father's map and some parts of our mother's map, each with hand-me-down genes from all of their ancestors before them.

The bits that join together are random. It's as though all of the maps have been torn into little pieces and thrown back together again. The pieces fall together by chance to make a new pattern with a unique map for you.

After we are born, the people and events in the world around us influence our inner map, changing or rearranging the details. All the while, our inner map guides us on how to behave, think, and act.

But our ancestors didn't know everything. They couldn't teach us what they didn't know. When we see only a small piece of the earth at one time or hear only the ideas of one people who were taught in one way, we think narrowly and see a flat world.

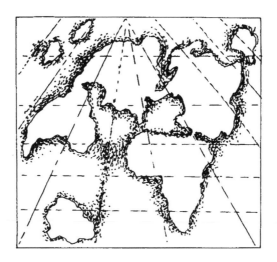

We do things that follow our ancestors' inner mind maps. The history of great thinkers shows how our minds touch one another with shared knowledge no one creates alone.

Ignorance can be our enemy. But we can turn it into our friend by letting it spur us on to learning and discovery and wisdom.

As we grow and follow our inner map, we may have an experience that reveals something about us we never before realized. Maybe we're not so honest or we're braver than we thought.

Be honest with yourself about who you are and why you might have trouble understanding others. Listening to other people's stories takes us beyond old, familiar boundaries called beliefs, to a feeling for the wideness of the world. That feeling can spark new ideas, so our differences make a good fit working together for greater results.

Facts just are (dogs bark, the house is there). Everything else is an opinion or belief (dogs make good pets, that is an ugly house). An inner idea map may have a fact or a belief that is shared by people who understand it in the same way; but not all people may have been taught this way. For example, a belief might be that everybody should have a dog for a pet.

We all carry beliefs that are based on our past experiences —
what we did or what happened to us or what others told us.
But those beliefs hold us back from thinking in a new way
that might work better for us. We get the chance to discover
a new, better way when change comes into our lives.

At times we may feel scared and afraid of the unknown that lies ahead. Courage does not exist without fear. These forces are natural. They're like friendly ghosts that haunt, urging us to explore new boundaries. Living in our world is like having a messy room that we just can't seem to straighten up. We may like a lot of order in our lives. But sometimes, no matter what we do, disorder enters our lives with unexpected events. Chaos haunts us all until we get a wider understanding of the world and our place in it. That understanding lets us see the order in the chaos or the reason behind what has happened.

Trying something new and then being rejected or failing at it can also stop us, unless we are curious and never give up.

Worries jam up when everyday habits aren't getting us the results we want.

Doing what we always have done no longer works, so we consider new ideas, the unknown. But not knowing can be scary. Our ancestors survived fear by stepping out of gummed up beliefs and behaving in new ways, discovering imagination had something to say to them. Having no worries could be our greatest worry, keeping us stuck in the old ways.

With the confidence to discover new paths, we begin new journeys into the unknown with joy instead of fear.

When you don't like being rushed to change or take risks, stop to think calmly for a moment about you instead of what you're being asked to do. Picture brave, bright parts of you. Remember to say "I want to" instead of "I have to" and make the positive move that cheers you onward.

A Better Way

Spending time pondering your natural talents helps you solve your problems. Remember where you have come from and think about who you are becoming.

Let go of angry old thoughts. We all have to figure out a better way to get along, and staying angry doesn't help. You may want someone else to explain what to do about the hurt feelings you don't understand. If you don't talk about your problem, others may not realize how hurt and confused you are.

Other people grow up in worlds very different from your own. What is different seems scary until you make the effort to understand, then it's awesome to see the odds you can overcome.

Moving into Change

Sometimes we may be afraid of what we don't yet know. When we're unwilling to face fear, we stay stuck. We don't do anything to get over our fear and only think about how scared we are. But simply singing or moving can make us feel better by changing the way we feel. And when we feel better we can tackle what we thought we were afraid of.

The should's, ought's, have to's, and "Yes, dear, you can do anything you want to do, as long as you do what WE want you to!" make us angry and afraid. They have become fearsome symbols in songs, masks, stories, dances, and drawings, showing up as roaring lions, hidden dragons, crouching monsters, or things that go bump in the night.

When you safely talk with someone who listens well, you can improve your courage by facing your fears. You can confidently tell your monsters to get a new job somewhere far away from you!

New Ideas Replace Old Problems

Maybe old ideas come between you and others. We may pretend that we are comfortable, but we should pay attention and listen to the lonely, hurt, worried feelings that we bottle up inside.

Some do not want to change at all and never look into the root values of understanding, order, freedom, and harmony. But we can learn how to solve our own problems by looking at them.

When your talent is needed, it brings confidence to your actions in a natural way. Confident, you remember all you were meant to be and can still become, even as some parts of your maps— inside or outside— are changing.

It's Safe to Be Different

Each person may be suited to some tasks more than others. We want to decide for ourselves what to think, feel, say, do, and believe so we can do these activities that come easiest to us — and often are the most fun. But we also want to join others in what we do and be close to each other.

Sometimes, getting along with others isn't easy without help because we are so different. Everyone needs to understand why a task that is easy for neat Thinkabouts (like keeping a desk organized) is so difficult for messy Talkabouts (it's here, somewhere; we file by pile).

We can learn to forgive other's mistakes and let go of fear of being different or trying something new or working with others who are different. First though, we need to feel safe. We need to feel secure enough that we can talk about our worries instead of stuffing things inside. When we feel safe, then we can bravely take on our fears.

Things to Do: Find a Hero

Once in a while, someone comes along and the story they live inspires generations that come after. Those people become heroes to us, reminding us of all we were meant to be and can still become. They might be someone who dares to act upon what they know is right, like Sojourner Truth did when she guided slaves to freedom. They might overcome great physical handicaps like Evelyn Glennie did when she became an award-winning percussionist in spite of being deaf. Or maybe it is some person you know who has shown you how to be true to yourself.

If we change peoples' minds, we change the world. Find a great thinker whose style is most like yours. What would you like most to do? Who are your heroes, and how do they seem heroic to you? Is your purpose similar to theirs?

Ask a hundred children to draw Jack and his beanstalk and they will all draw it differently and they will all draw it correctly, because it's what they see inside that matters most.

If you were all alone in the universe with no one to talk to, no one with which to share the beauty of the stars, to laugh with, to touch, what would be your purpose in life? It is other life, it is love, which gives your life meaning. This is harmony. We must discover the joy of each other, the joy of challenge, the joy of growth.

— Mitsugi Saotome:

Synergy Pals Profile:
Understanding each other

Learn to Use All of Your Natural Talents
Thinkabout Practices Carefully
Lookabout Pictures Success
Feelabout Tugs Hearts
Talkabout Inspires Ideas

Thinkabout Owl
- I need time to figure it out.
- I feel cornered and stubborn when you push or criticize me.
- Because I value order and conformity, I need a quiet, safe place to work and play.

Lesson for Owls: I reflect at my best and am critical at my worst. I can learn to RISK starting without rules or all of the facts, SHARE my feelings and be kind to others, STRETCH my boundaries for just having fun.

Feelabout Koala
- I need to be part of the group.
- I feel left out when what I feel doesn't seem to matter.
- Because I value harmony, I need to be a part of whatever is going on.

Lesson for Koalas: I serve others at my best and am stern at my worst. I can learn to RISK being honest about my needs and feelings, SHARE my decisions, expectations, and dreams, STRETCH to challenge myself and take charge.

Lookabout Lion
- I need to act on my plans and direct things.
- I feel blocked and angry when you avoid decisions and follow-through actions.
- Because I value my freedom to act, I need to do new things and get results.

Lesson for Lions: I am decisive at my best and defiant at my worst. I can learn to RISK being fun-loving while working more slowly, SHARE by listening to others' feelings and ideas, STRETCH to be more considerate and accepting of others.

Talkabout Chimp
- I need to question and communicate.
- I feel misunderstood when others don't listen to my inspired ideas or share my playful mood.
- Because I value understanding, I need to direct myself and question the rules.

Lesson for Chimps: I am invigorating at my best and scattered at my worst. I can learn to RISK losing inspiration by being more organized, SHARE the work, STRETCH to plan ahead and finish work with quality.

Exploring Further: Work Styles

Discuss how you feel about the different responses to the unfinished statement below. Which do you identify with most? Least? Why?

I work best when I can...

...work with others and be shown how to do things by someone who knows how. Feelabout.

...think and work quietly on my own, following directions step by step. Thinkabout.

...watch what someone does well, plan how I will do it, and get it done. Lookabout.

...tell others my new ideas, inspiring them to risk doing things in a new way. Talkabout.

Chapter 6

I Love the Me I See in You

Life Stories

Things to Do:
Who Do You Think You Are?

Synergy Pals Profile:
Easy for Me, Easy for You

Exploring Further:
Difficult Tasks

Life Stories

Each life is an original story we write ourselves.

Our life stories tell about our growth, our feelings, our choices, and our changes inside as our outside world changes—sometimes pleasantly, sometimes painfully.

Every person who ever lived in any place and time in the whole world takes the journey of life.

Certain parts of the journey (like growing up) are the same for everyone. Having the same experience as others connects us and lets us see ourselves in them. Then we form bonds and treat each other well.

Some parts of the journey may be hard (or even scary). Fear can stop us, but we can overcome fear and keep going, learning our lessons. These become our stories, chapters in our life story. The adventures we have—good or bad—and how we behave and think shape who we are.

Our core values, our inner maps, guide us on these adventures. They are like landmarks on a path that tell us what to do in any situation.

When we have an experience that we really love, that seems perfect for us, we have reached a destination of sorts. Our heart tells us this is important, we remember it, place an X on our inner map, and return to it often. Like our core values, these special times give us ideas of who we are and who or what we might become.

If we feel lost and confused, it may be our heart telling us we are following someone else's inner map. This new situation might not match our own needs and wishes. It may feel as if others say and do things in a way we don't consider important.

Each of us can use the inner map to open a doorway to our own life journey. Others' inner maps are good for them but may not help us find our way. Pay attention to your unique way of looking at the world with certain thoughts, feelings, behaviors, and interests. Your own inner map will return you to a comfortable and familiar path.

Some people have inner maps so different from ours we hardly recognize we're on the same path. But great adventures in life can happen when we open ourselves up to understanding people with inner maps very different from our own while we stay true to who we are.

Other people have inner maps so much like ours it seems we can read their minds, and it feels as if we've known them forever.

Whether our inner maps are opposites or similar each of us discovers life in our own way. We are guided by our thoughts and feelings every day of our lives, each of us using our senses in different ways to find out the activities we enjoy most.

The discoveries and choices along the way are always interesting. Think about an activity that you resist learning in order to avoid pain. Is this activity too slow, too fast, too demanding, too easy, too detailed, too hands-on, or too risky? We feel pleased when we overcome a challenge.

Things To Do: Who Do You Think You Are?

Read about the different Synergy Pals around the tree stump below. The traits of one animal Pal may sound just like you. Some things about you hardly ever change. Those things are your core values and they are what cause you to think and act the way you do and to be who you are. We all need and do different things: to serve, to get results, to have action, and to express ideas.

Color rings in the section of the tree by the Synergy Pal most like you. Use that Pal's color.

Thinkabout Owl needs to serve others
• Values order
• Focuses on inside thoughts
• Needs to work on having fun!
GREEN

Lookabout Lion needs to get results
• Values freedom
• Is very direct
• Needs to work on considering feelings!
BLUE

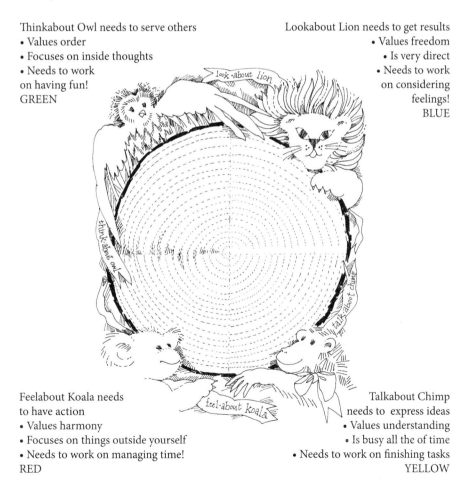

Feelabout Koala needs to have action
• Values harmony
• Focuses on things outside yourself
• Needs to work on managing time!
RED

Talkabout Chimp needs to express ideas
• Values understanding
• Is busy all the of time
• Needs to work on finishing tasks
YELLOW

Synergy Pals Profile:
Easy for Me, Easy for You

What is easy for you to do? What is hard? When do you feel most alive? The Synergy Pals can give you insight to what is easy and what is hard for you to do.

Look at the chart on the next page and think about what you like to do. Do you prefer to watch or to tell? Color the part of the horizontal bar that matches what you like to do—the left part of the bar if you prefer to watch, the right side of the bar if you prefer to tell.

How about to think and to feel? Which is more like you? Color half of the vertical bar that is you—the top half to think or the bottom half to feel.

Look at the section bounded by your colored bars. Do some of these activities match what you like to do?

THINK-WATCH

Thinkabout activities
- **Assemble a model plane by reading instructions**
- **Walk instead of ride**
- **Organize your room and desk schedule**
- **Be exactly on time all day**
- **Make an A-B-C to-do list**
- **Think about ways to recycle**

WATCH-TELL

Lookabout activities
- Plan and start a project
- Talk to an expert
- Learn how to use a new computer program
- Write and direct a play
- Move a plan into action
- Read about something you enjoy

Think

Watch

Tell

Feelabout activities
- Ride a roller coaster
- Use touch to compose a piece of music, dance, or art
- Explain what you learned about a sad memory
- Act quickly in an emergency
- Make something that lasts
- Dance to music

FEEL-WATCH

Talkabout activities
- **Take part in a sand castle contest**
- **Discover the hidden meaning in a totem**
- **March in a parade**
- **Perform in front of others**
- **Share your daydreams**
- **Talk about a better world**
- **Challenge old ideas with new discoveries**

Feel

FEEL-TELL

Activities in one square may be easy for you. See if you can discover how to do things that are hard for you. Could you do an action from a different activity square?

You've identified one square that's a lot like you. Is a second square like you, too, but not as much? Which one? Lookabout? Talkabout? Feelabout? Thinkabout? These two are a little different, and their differences could give you problems. Thinkabout wants safety and Talkabout wants change. How could your two choices make you argue with yourself?

Think of something you don't like to do. What square is it in or would it be in on the chart on the previous page? Choose to do one thing in this square. Notice that it can be fun to try something new. Doing activities that are not easy for you helps you grow more comfortable with coping with changes that life brings you.

Exploring Further: Difficult Tasks

See how you feel about the statements below. Which is most like you? Least? Why? What do others think about you? Why do we each choose something different? Ask your friends and family for friendly feedback.

Sometimes it's hard for me to...

…risk a quarrel by telling the truth about how I feel because if I hurt someone's feelings Harmony goes away.

Feelabout Koala may feel left out, keeping the peace at all costs, longing to be part of what's going on.

Lesson for Koalas: Learn to get going.

…finish the things I start when I'm excited about something new because I'll miss Understanding a different, newer idea.

Talkabout Chimp may feel misunderstood, wanting others to be open to new approaches while solving old problems.

Lesson for Chimps: Learn to finish old tasks before starting new ones.

…be gentle and considerate of other's feelings because I'll lose the Freedom to get where I want to go.

Lookabout Lion may feel blocked when others need him most because he doesn't see what good others offer.

Lesson for Lions: Learn to be sensitive to feelings as well as words.

…make decisions when I don't know the facts because I'll risk the Order I need to feel safe.

Thinkabout Owl may feel cornered and doubtful when criticized, starting without the rules or all of the facts.

Lesson for Owls: Plan on taking some safe risks for more fun.

Chapter 7
Soul Stories

The Story of Our Lives

Things to Do:
Write a Story

Synergy Pals Profile:
Story Preferences

Exploring Further:
Stories

The Story of Our Lives

Our beliefs about who we are, how we fit into the world, and what our promise is are really only stories that we tell ourselves. But they are among the most powerful forces in our lives. And these stories begin in childhood with the first comments from others: "What a pretty girl you are" or "What a smart boy."

Stories Find Our Common Voices

People understand the world through stories that touch their deepest values. Shared stories are remarkably similar around the world. Human Stories repeat as if they had never happened before. All story creations are always about transformation.

We long to hear stories about order, understanding, freedom, and harmony. The storyteller expands our world with these universal ideas. Our heads and hearts listen to what interests us most, such as stories about friendship, mission, and adventure. Stories remind us of things we care about or things that scare us. Stories bring us closer to our roots, to what is most important to us, to our values.

Wisdom

Stories are a very important way to search for wise answers to our struggles in life. The loving voice of the storyteller gives us stories with problems similar to our own—and with solutions. When we recognize our problems in the stories, we can benefit from the wisdom in those lessons.

Wisdom helps us find lessons in everything we do. We understand stories that we have heard many times. When we hear new stories and connect them to the old stories, we add to our wisdom and revise our inner maps. Learning from the past is a miracle of time speeded up as we discover new answers.

We may be curious, seeking to find out more. If we are clear about what we want to learn from the start, we can gain much, even from our mistakes.

Changing Our Inner Maps

Our inner map is our very own view of the world we live in. As our world changes around us, our inner maps and our ancestors' rules help us make sense of those changes to adapt and thrive. The wisdom in our ancestors' stories can help us to choose our destinations, face obstacles, chase fear, seek forgiveness, and picture success.

Our thoughts may tell us things are so-o-o-o good, but our feelings might tell us something different. When our hearts speak in this way, it is to help us find healing and wholeness. Even though we might want change, we can still feel sad as we let go of old ways or worn-out ideas.

It may be hard to see how to begin to change anything at all what with thoughts and feelings all saying something different, but with stories to guide us, one idea can turn into an action that makes a big change on our inner map.

Turning on the Light

Our stories contain the memory of who we are and tell us about our need to begin something new. When we want to discover how to grow, our hearts turn on a light that helps us look Inside. The light asks, "What can I learn from this experience? If I make this choice, what happens?" A little step leads to a bigger step of connecting ideas. A very small change of heart and behavior can make a very large change in our purpose and destiny.

Stories are a way of looking at our ancestors' ideas. If we look back far enough, we see how everything goes around in cycles of growth and decay. Problems arise and then are solved, just as they were in ages past. And in each one of us, we see a new story growing—problems and solutions, challenges and victories, fears and advancements—forever moving in full circle and creating our wonderful self.

Myth

Myths are ways to explain the world, to put order in what seems like chaos, to show how we fit in the big, wide world. But myths are based upon how the myth-makers see the world.

If we see differently—maybe because of new discoveries—the old myths may no longer apply. But we become more tolerant of differences as we see that myths suit the people that believed them at the time. Changing minds change the world. We see a new story forever growing.

The world now is much different from the one in which you and your parents were born. And change continues. There are always new ways of seeing the world. But what stays constant is our heart speaking our truth, reminding us of what is most important to us in the creative circle of love.

Our beliefs about how we fit into the world are really only stories. But they are the most powerful forces in our lives and they begin in childhood, with language.

Language affects the nervous system of this thinking world and fills up our senses.

We use language to describe the world we know, but language also influences the way we know the world. We might be afraid of bees, but when we know that bees aren't interested in us (unless we're flowers), our story about bees changes.

If we learn to name our feelings, we can also learn to change any negative feelings we have. Then conflict can lead to cooperation as we forgive one and all. Then the story gets a happy ending for all those around us. Only the heart knows the correct way to see round when others see a flat world view.

Sometimes we do foolish things to feel smart or run from something that isn't after us. Some of us need to belong, to feel confident, to succeed, or to change the world. As we adapt and stretch our understanding, we can see common threads in every story. That is how myths, legends, and stories embrace us all to tell us about the world as we grow up.

Fear comes from being in conflict without being able to resolve it, which causes mischief and misunderstanding. Our inner maps and stories old and new show us rules to send fear away. Like magic, stories take an idea—what is invisible, just sitting in our mind—and show us how to make it visible with action.

Our ancestors' stories contain the wisdom of all ages, holding the common thread of being alive, being alike, and wanting the same things. As we stretch a bit further, we see our common roots as one story of the heart of the world.

I love the me I see in you.

Things To Do: Write a Story

Stories tell us to learn something from what we do. When we understand how to think things over in a new way, we may change the meanings of our history.

Imagining things may bring about an unlikely journey. For example, one man who was afraid of dogs as a child, learned about them, imagined the world through a dog's mind, and then became a friend of dogs everywhere.

Write about one important day in your life using the sentence below. Most stories ever written or told can be reduced to this one long sentence. You will notice what you value by telling your own story. Everything good that was ever written has at its core some basic human value, or the lack of a basic value. This can make you think about what you would value if you lost it. Examples are love, freedom, trust, courage.

Sentence:
Once upon a time something happened to a person (the incident) and he decided that he would pursue a goal (the prize), so he invented a plan of action (the strategy) and even though there were forces trying to stop him (the conflict) he moved forward because there was a lot at stake (the stakes); and just as things seemed to get as bad as they could (the worst moment), he learned an important lesson (the lesson), and when offered the prize, he had to decide whether or not to take it (the decision); and in making that decision he filled a need that had been created by something in his past that made life bleak and sad (the real story).

Example:

Once upon a time, a young woman saw wonderful drawings in a book (the incident) and she decided to practice drawing until she could make pictures like that (the prize), so she practiced everyday (the strategy) and even though she had a job that required working into the night (the conflict), she moved forward because drawing made her happy (the stakes); and just when she felt so exhausted giving her time to drawing and to her demanding job (the worst moment), she learned how important drawing was to her (the lesson), and she had to decide whether to keep drawing or find another job (the decision); and when she decided to keep drawing, she found that she could tell a story with her pictures that made other people happy, which made her happy because she always wanted to help people (and herself) to be less sad and more glad (the real story).

Synergy Pals Profile: Story Preferences

WATCH

TELL

Thinkabout Owl: Structured

Likes stories with characters who are dedicated and loyal and who behave appropriately. Likes stories about family safety and security. Likes words about concrete things.

Natural systems/ecology

Lookabout Lion: Independent

Likes stories about exploration of universal principles. Wants to know the whys of the world and likes strong, independent characters who are great thinkers. Likes explorers and the study of societies and science. Needs to know concepts.

Engineering/building/quantum physics

Feelabout Koala: Active

Likes romance and fantasy stories where characters have strong romantic images. Likes stories of love, everlasting values, and happy endings. Likes lots of action and functional, concrete words.

Psychology

Talkabout Chimp: Interactive

Likes creativity and adventure stories with characters who are spontaneous risk takers. A reformer is always protesting and creating new ways of being. Likes imagination and imagery and thinking outside the box!

Mythology

FEEL

Exploring Further: Stories

Discuss the different statements below. Which do you like the most? Least? Why? Add your favorites.

I like stories about . . .

...real-life problems that end happily, tugging our hearts to like one another better (*Sarah Plain and Tall* and *Heidi*). Feelabout

...true adventures with skilled heroes/heroines who make things happen (*Other Side of the Mountain* and *Black Beauty*). Thinkabout

...ingenious thinkers from history or fiction whose knowledge leads tomorrow (*Helen Keller* and *Star Wars*). Lookabout

...inspiring new ideas, magical things, and faraway places (*Wizard of Oz* and *A Wrinkle in Time*). Talkabout

Chapter 8

Give and Take

What Inspires You?

How Can You Tell How Others Feel?

Things to Do:
Reading Each Other

Synergy Pals Profile:
Skills to Share

Exploring Further:
Communication

What Inspires You?

How Can You Tell How Others Feel?

When you are with your family, or friends, or other people, how do you know what they are feeling? Do you watch their faces and how they move to see what they feel? Do you listen to their voices and how they talk to hear what they feel? Do you listen to their words for information that explains how they feel? Do you touch their hands or hug them to sense what they feel?

When we know what others are feeling, working with them can be fun and rewarding. Others teach you things you feel you need to learn, holding your hand or paying attention to what you need to learn. Support feels good because it gives us a safe place to try new ways of doing.

Many Faces, One Heart

But working with others can also be challenging because we are all so different.

A Feelabout likes to work and play with action, a Lookabout works with experience and ideas, a Thinkabout works a skilled job that lasts, and a Talkabout works with others to help them create dreams and better their best. All Synergy Pals contribute different and important parts to a team. Figuring out how to work together makes a great team.

Discuss what basic teamwork rules might be. Focus on needs; yours, others, and the whole team's. Without knowing your needs and taking care of them, you will waste time and energy on unimportant matters, and not feel fulfilled. Discuss how to focus your self-confidence, listen to your own needs, and then match them up with the team's needs.

Sensations: What does each person see, hear, feel, taste, smell, touch, imagine differently? How does each show outside what is being experienced inside?

Interpretations: What is each one's thoughts, opinions, beliefs, attitudes, and facts?

Motivation and Intentions: How does each express him/herself?

Feelings: What is each one's feelings? How does each find the meaning in mistakes?

Actions: Describe the behaviors each sees and their impact on feelings and situations.

Words: A word is used as a symbol for an experience. Word choices may be positive or negative. What words are spoken and written by each?

Which Synergy Pal are you most like?

Lookabout Lion: I see what you're saying. I see your point. I share your vision.

Feelabout Koala: How do you feel about that? Stay in touch! Let's move on the vital concepts.

Talkabout Chimp: I am tuning that out. I hear what you're saying.

Thinkabout Owl: Please help me figure this out. Think it over.

The Roots of the Grandmother Tree

What comes naturally to you, that's easy for you to do and that you like doing?

Things I Like: Every Which Way

Doing big projects   Looking at nature

Getting ideas

Making a toy

Playing in the water

Talking with friends

Dressing up   Reading a book

Building a fort   Riding a bike

Making people laugh

Playing music

Sharing a secret

Feeding a baby

Camping out   Painting a picture

Solving problems

Dancing to music

Making cookies

Drawing a plan

Being with animals   Planting a garden

Playing sports

Watching the stars

Talking with grandparents

Gathering flowers

Singing in harmony

Thinking about everything

Fixing a bike, step by step

Taking care of a baby

Playing with clay

Reading a good book

What interests you most? If you were going to tell someone something special about yourself, what would it be? What comes naturally to you that's easy to do and that you like doing? These are your gifts, what you give when you work with others.

When you know what truly interests you, you'll understand more about yourself and feel good about sharing your gifts with others.

You'll become the person you were meant to be, both Outside and Inside. You'll understand how to get along with others, how you figure things out, what you can do to get things done, who listens to your questions and ideas.

No one else in the world is just like YOU. That's what "unique" means. Just one in the whole world, in the whole universe.

Thank you for understanding I don't have to be perfect for you to love me.

Only YOU look, think, talk, move, feel, and see the world the way you do.

Things to Do: Reading Each Other

When working in teams, we have to learn how others are doing with their tasks, and this often means learning about what others on the team are feeling. Discuss these questions:

How do you show others what you are feeling?

What do you need when you are upset?

Do you know how to ask for help?

What makes you angry?

Do you know when your values are being met?

Things to Do: The Power of Team Building

We feel most comfortable doing what comes easiest to us, using our natural talents. Just knowing this will keep us from flying blind. Be realistic about the jobs you take on; make sure they match your talents, at least in part. The same is true for the jobs you give to people with different talents. We grow, learn, give, and take with others in spite of and because of our differences. The following list are some things to know about yourself when you start to team up to get something done.

1) What is most important to you in work or play?

2) What needs to happen to get the results you want?

3) Do you need help solving the problem?

4) Do you know how to solve the problem at all?

5) What you want to do least is the skill you need most.

The following are categories of problems, from easy to impossible.

- Easy tasks are those we can finish alone.

- More difficult ones need help from others to break the problem into simpler parts we can solve,

- Impossible ones are beyond our task-solving abilities

Synergy Pals Profile:
Skills to Share

Thinkabout Seeks Order
Needs to serve. Likes to ask, listen, watch and avoids risk.

Feelabout Seeks Harmony
Needs action. Likes to create, relate, and sympathize.

Lookabout Seeks Freedom
Needs results. Likes to know, choose, and plan actions.

Talkabout Seeks Understanding
Needs ideas. Likes to show, tell, and express.

Which way of being or action in the chart following best describe you? For example, if you were in a play, which role would you choose: Thinkabout, Lookabout, Talkabout, or Feelabout? Circle your first choice for each subject in the chart.

Activity Chart

Subject	Thinkabout	Lookabout	Talkabout	Feelabout
A play	Details	Control	Expression	Motion
A kite	Facts	Plans	Possibilities	Hands-on
Your room	Tidy	Visual	Unique	Cozy
Am helped by	Specifics	Experts	Enthusiasm	Friendliness
A report	Data	Development	Imagination	Acting out
Time sense	Punctual	Mastery	Courteous	Spontaneous
Learns from	Practice	Experience	Discovery	Action

Exploring Further: Communications

Although you have one preference for each subject, all four actions work together to make a successful activity. That's why teamwork is so important. Other team members bring their different preferred contributions to the activity so that all needed actions are in place. We feel good when these actions or ways of being, all of equal importance, make the team.

Discuss how you feel about the different responses to the unfinished statement below. Which do you identify with most? Least? Why? Discuss how and why we each choose a different response.

When I'm with others talking and listening, I...

...First watch and listen, then feel free to explain the plan I see and what to do.

...First enthusiastically share my new ideas, then want to hear if they understood me.

...Warmly ask about their feelings and share my feelings in a friendly, helpful way.

...Politely listen until I'm asked what I think, then I quietly answer.

Chapter 9

Nature's Cycles

Finding Patterns

Things to Do:
Setting and Achieving Goals

Things to Do:
Roots and Branches

Synergy Pal's Profile:
Problem Solving

Exploring Further:
Problem Solving…

Finding Patterns

Nature's story circles continuously turn around in world history. Echoing in from the past, the bones of the same story and what happens today and what will go on tomorrow. Your family is a circle of people that love you within the seasons of time, good and bad, as babies cry, teens tease, lovers kiss, elders gray. Your children grow up and have children of their own. Circling times meet, then come and go again in changing patterns. We see time at work in Nature's cycles: Sunrise turns to sunset; flowers bud, bloom, produce seeds; spring turns to summer, then fall, then winter, and back to spring again. Passing time brings change, and many changes follow a pattern.

Time is always making changes and ticking in our heads. And each passing second, minute, hour holds so many possibilities. How will we use our time — for good or wasted? When we know better, we do better. It's time to make the most of who we are.

When we are having the time of our lives, we shout victory, and our bodies feel joy. When we find a list of things we were supposed to do but didn't, we feel defeated or upset. When we make the most of our time, we feel good about ourself.

Past and present successes and mistakes connect us to important ideas over and over. Old and new stories loop backwards and forwards, history echoing up to now and into the future. If you look, you might see a pattern to your history, making the same kinds of mistakes over and over or using your talents to bring you success. We begin to see patterns in our stories, and we can learn from them. Sometimes we can change the ones that aren't working for us, the ones that bring results we don't like.

But some patterns can be very hard to change. For instance, you might feel tip-top first thing in the morning while your brother feels most energetic after lunch. Some people like to stay up late at night. Patterns like those can be very hard to change.

Some patterns are easier to change. Our behavior patterns — the way we act in the world — show us our own ways to understand the world and get information for our inner maps. There is no best way. If you know your behavior patterns you can adapt them to meet new needs.

Some of the most important questions you can ask yourself are: Do my actions bring me the results I need in the long run? How do my actions and my needs fit together? Do I have patterns of behaving that work for me?

Acting out of anger can be a pattern that doesn't work for us. Anger is a natural feeling expressing hurt; it is not a behavior. If we understand our angry feelings, we can behave in healthy — not angry — ways, using anger's lessons to solve problems with each other and be better friends.

When we accept and understand the lessons of life — within the lessons of anger — we can learn and grow in healthy ways. This is the path to our self-respect.

Things To Do: Roots and Branches

On the next page, you are looking down at the top of a tree. Its stability comes from the four root values, where they connect in the core.

Find your root value and put your name in the leaves growing there. Next, think about the people you live with — your family and friends.

Put each one's name in a group of leaves growing from the root value (order, freedom, understanding, and harmony) you think best applies to him or her. Next, draw branches to connect you with each of them.

Draw strong branches to the people you feel close to, those who listen and understand you most. Draw thinner branches to those who don't know you very well. Draw broken branches to those with whom you have troubles.

Forever Growing Deeply Rooted Values

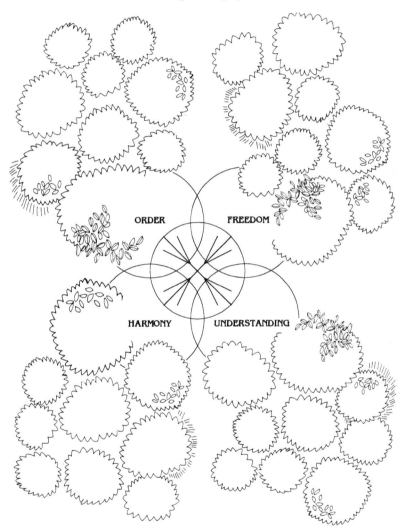

*Birds build their nests in circles,
for theirs is the same religion as ours.*

—Black Elk

Things to Do: Setting and Achieving Goals

Setting and achieving goals are very specific ways to solve your problems and get what you need. They are easy to do when you know how.

1. List three specific things you want. Examples are: getting a computer, buying a bicycle, going to camp.

2. Circle the most important of your three wants.

3. Go though the process under Synergy Pals Profile: Problem Solving on page 137 to make a plan for getting what you want.

4. Find someone who is already getting the results you want. Find out what that person is doing. Doing the same thing (only in your own way) will get the same results if you follow through.

Some questions lead us to better answers and help us find a way to act that feels right.

1. Focus. What is the most important thing to me now? That is called the result you want.

2. How would I like to get the result I want?

3. What three steps do I have to take now to make the things happen that will get the result I want?

4. Everyday make a to-do list in three columns, ranked by their importance to you.

5. Ask yourself if your actions last week were "on purpose." Did you do the things from your list?

*To accomplish great things,
we must not only act, but also dream;
not only plan, but also believe.*

— Anatole France:

ORDER

Skill Master
4. Present facts
5. Be prepared

FREEDOM

Vision Leader
6. Plan and follow-
through

Purpose Owner
1. Know my wants

Peacemaker
7. Keep things in
harmony

Dream Mover
2. Brainstorm
3. Be optimistic

HARMONY

UNDERSTANDING

Synergy Pals Profile: Problem-Solving

PURPOSE OWNER
Know my wants: This is my present heartfelt purpose, what I value most right now. I am responsible for wanting, getting, and having this.

DREAM MOVER
Brainstorm: Visit the Understanding Talkabout Chimp box and write down ideas about what I want. Anything goes.

Be optimistic: List the very best that can happen with these ideas.

SKILL MASTER
Present the facts: Visit the Order Thinkabout Owl box and list seven facts: cost, size, requirements, time available, obstacles, whatever you know that is not an opinion. Note: "I deserve this" is an opinion.

Be prepared: List the worst and most unsafe things about the facts. Accept realistic limitations of tasks and skills.

VISION LEADER
Plan and follow-through: Visit the Freedom Lookabout Lion box and list one clear plan of action and follow it through. Be time specific and say by when you will make it happen. Accept limitations of human nature.

PEACEMAKER
Keep things in harmony: Visit the Harmony Feelabout Koala box and answer the following questions: Does this course of action really feel okay? Does it seem most right for me and for everyone? Be flexible and adapt to change.

If the answer is NO, check your Feelabout Koala intuition to repeat the process. If YES, go ahead and take action.

Exploring Further: Problem Solving

Discuss how you feel about the different responses to the unfinished statement below. Which do you identify with most? Least? Why? Discuss how and why we each choose a different response.

I solve my problems or make decisions best when . . .

. . . I brainstorm with others, trust hunches, discover a new way to put ideas together (Talkabout Chimp, the Dream Mover).

. . . I know the facts that tell me exactly what to do to get the right answer (Thinkabout Owl, the Skill Master).

. . . I plan things my own way by comparing good and bad ideas to get quick results (Lookabout Lion, the Vision Leader).

. . . I feel safe enough working with a group to ask other people to help me (Feelabout Koala, the Peacemaker).

Chapter 10

Home Sweet Home

Celebrating Our Safe Homes —
Near and Far

Things to Do:
Sing Your Own Song

Synergy Pals Profile:
Song

Celebrating Our Safe Homes—Near and Far

Where you live has a lot to do with how you feel and think, what you see and do. How are you different from others? Sometimes you might want to live somewhere else. Have you always lived in one place? Or have you lived in many places?

Think about where you live. What do you like best about it? What is special on the Outside, such as favorite playgrounds? What is special on the Inside, such as good memories? Which is your favorite room and why? What are the colors you like best? The shapes? The sounds? The smells? Draw the memories you have of this special room using vivid colors. Feelings come to us from the memories of our own homes.

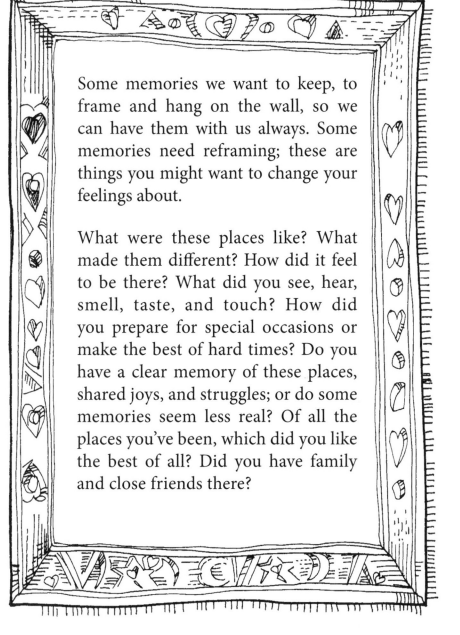

Some memories we want to keep, to frame and hang on the wall, so we can have them with us always. Some memories need reframing; these are things you might want to change your feelings about.

What were these places like? What made them different? How did it feel to be there? What did you see, hear, smell, taste, and touch? How did you prepare for special occasions or make the best of hard times? Do you have a clear memory of these places, shared joys, and struggles; or do some memories seem less real? Of all the places you've been, which did you like the best of all? Did you have family and close friends there?

Take a walk around your neighborhood. On your walk, find something that interests you. How do you feel in your favorite place? What do you like least about your neighborhood? What do you like most?

Our Patchwork Families

Do you live with many people or just a few?

Have you always been part of the same family? Or are you part of more than one family?

Think about the people with whom you live. Who listens to you? Who understands you? Who appreciates you just the way you are?

Who are your friends — the people you like to spend time with?

Our friends and neighbors are sometimes like a large family to us. Do you have neighbors you like a lot? Have you found like-minded friends who become as close to you as brothers or sisters?

This is a circle of people who care about you. This loving circle makes us feel safe as we find where we belong. Within this circle we are strong and we find our place at the table.

How do you honor your elders for the wisdom of their years? It makes a difference when someone understands what you are going through from cradle to grave. Birth and death are part of the same cycle.

Heart Strings Tie Us Together

All through life people around us pay attention to special days. This brings back faces and names and feelings that make a positive difference for us. We open our eyes to a treasure quest of our love and caring in life.

We also join together with others to help overcome challenges. Where there's help there's hope. Caring people who assist us make us more than we were.

When someone you know is hurting, just letting them know that you care about them helps them feel better. It makes a difference when someone understands what you're going through and offers support.

We can feel very loved or very alone — sometimes both at the same time. Being alone does not have to be lonely. You can always rely on and understand yourself, even if you don't understand the changes that are taking place around you. When we want to discover what's Inside, our hearts turn on a light that helps us look Inside and understand our inner maps, to wisely choose our destinations.

Wherever you go, there's a whole Friendly Universe to explore, Outside and Inside.

It's All about You

People sing to celebrate important events in their lives. They feel less alone gathering with others for praise and special days.

In songs we feel the different rhythms of our time and culture: order, freedom, understanding, and harmony. Look at a list of new and old songs with your parents or a grown-up. What values do you feel expressed in the old songs? In the new? Have they changed over the years?

Things to Do: Sing Your Own Song

Write a "soul song," a story from your life set to song, keeping the words simple — the simpler, the better. Use the tune from a song you know or stick with basic chords and avoid tricky rhythms. That way, you can remember it wherever you are — in the shower on the way to school, in the car. Teach and record the song if you can, maybe with a group.

What traditions, instruments, sounds, beats, tempos, tunes, and lyrics come to mind? Make up your own list of Synergy Pals songs to sing and celebrate with your family.

Do you understand how songs about love and troubles make us feel what's important to us? When someone you know is hurting, words can soothe or hurt. Hope makes us feel stronger and able to carry on. Disappointment makes us feel sad because we seek something we never quite reach. Joy comes from doing things right. We join together overcoming challenges or celebrating good times. Songs can express these feelings many of which are linked closely with tender memories. We move onward, away from rejection or fear and toward a way of life truly loving others.

Exploring Further: Songs

THINK

Thinkabout Owl:
Songs of Order

Tradition
Fiddler on the Roof
Step by Step
If I had a Hammer
I'll Fly Away
I am a Rock
Sounds of Silence
He Was My Brother
From a Distance

Lookabout Lion:
Songs of Freedom

Hail to the Chief
Ain't No Mountain
High Enough
Born Free
Don't Fence Me In
My Way
Free to Be You and Me
I Am Woman

WATCH

TELL

Feelabout Koala:
Songs of Harmony

We are the World
Friends in Low Places
Achy-Breaky Heart
All You Need is Love
Love Me Tender
Don't Let Me Down
Danny Boy
Amazing Grace

Talkabout Chimp:
Songs of
Understanding

Imagine
Somewhere Over the
Rainbow
Dream the Impossible
Dream
It Could Have Been Me
Daydream Believer
Girls Just Want to Have Fun
50 Ways to Leave Your Lover

FEEL

*Mother Earth and her children are connected,
all working as one. Life is your adventure
in the circle of caring.*

Ardys Reverman

Chapter 11

Pulling Together

Understanding Myself and Others

Things to Do:
Seven Steps to Synergy

Synergy Pals Profile:
Core Needs

Exploring Further:
I Will Most Likely Do My Best Work...

Understanding Myself and Others

Synergy means the whole is greater than the sum of the parts. Individuals working together get far greater results than they would working separately on the same task. Each different natural talent is needed—a recipe where a group effort adds up to more than the separate pieces.

Synergy can happen more easily when we help each other understand how our differences naturally work together. If we play our parts well with others, we find an earth-friendly system and see much greater results.

How well do we live with diversity?

Working with others doesn't always bring synergistic results. Some combinations of talents and differences do not work well. For example, these things are not synergistic:

- ♥ Too much similarity = no creative action

- ♥ Too much difference = no agreement

- ♥ Too much misdirected natural talent = burnout

- ♥ Too few natural talents = frustration and anger

Things to Do: Seven Steps to Synergy

Use these steps to find out what work and play you want to do, what your heart says, what your strengths and weaknesses are, and the direction and steps to use to get what you want.

1. Know my needs. What do I want?

2. Brainstorm to inspire action. What are my best ideas?

3. Be optimistic. What are the best things that can happen?

4. Sort facts for safety. What are my risks?

5. Be prepared. What are the worst, most unsafe things that can happen?

6. Make up a plan for follow-through. What are my best ideas and facts? Move onward, overcome obstacles to focus energies.

7. Decide if the course of action feels okay. If it does, then you can go ahead. Does it feel wrong? Repeat the process from step 1.

I Can Understand Myself and Others Now

Now I can understand myself and others.

I know how I like best to do things and how I fit with others in the Friendly Universe. This is who we are.

I know now that change is okay, too.

I'm not afraid to learn new things, wonder, wander, stumble, or grow. I know it's perfectly all right to do something different if I want to. I use my talents well in ways that are fair to others.

If I have troubles, I know I always have a safe place within myself. My heart will always guide me. The wonder of life helps me feel the shared struggle and joy of working and belonging together. I give myself the freedom to be who I am.

When I understand myself, I understand my friends, too, because I see a bit of everyone in myself. That will make my journey through life an interesting trip.

All about us, the Friendly Universe nourishes and encourages us. How we act on ideas of order, freedom, understanding, and harmony turns the creative circle in the Friendly Universe, and it continues on and on.

You in the Universe

"A human being is a part of the whole, called by us 'Universe,' a part limited in time and space. He experiences himself, his thoughts and feelings as something separated from the rest — a kind of optical illusion of his consciousness. This delusion is a kind of prison for us, restricting us to our personal desire and to affection for a few persons nearest us. Our task must be to free ourselves from this prison by widening our circle of compassion to embrace all living creatures and the whole of nature in its beauty. Nobody is able to achieve this completely, but the striving for such achievement is itself a part of the liberation and foundation for inner security."

—Albert Einstein

Synergy Pals Profile: Core Needs

Thinkabout Owl
Skill Master

Facts (needs organization
to feel good)
- Looks at facts
- Lists facts
- Checks facts and
numbers
- Feels safe and sure
- Considers worst case

Lookabout Lion
Vision Leader

Planning (needs decision
to feel good)
- ♥ Takes calculated risks
- ♥ Follows through on
plan
- ♥ Gets expert advice
- ♥ Trusts knowledge and
competence

Action (needs action to
feel good)
- Feels good
- Connects all the parts
- Feels fulfilled
- Has synergy

Ideas (needs ideas to feel
good)
- ♥ Hatches terrific ideas
- ♥ Plans optimistically
- ♥ Has keen sixth sense
- ♥ Pictures future
success

Feelabout Koala
Peace Maker

Talkabout Chimp
Dream Mover

4 Ways to Make Sense of a "Whole" Idea

Exploring Further:

I Will Most Likely Do My Best Work...

...Practicing Carefully
Thinkabout Learners

- ♥ Want to do things "right" and by the book

- ♥ Strive for accuracy and quality, not quickness

- ♥ Look at a person's past as a key to trusting them in the future

- ♥ Want clearly-defined tasks, limited risk, and an "open door" policy

- ♥ Can be very creative in designing helpful systems if they are encouraged and allowed to work at their own pace

- ♥ Are good at taking things apart

- ♥ May worry quietly and criticize others when wronged

- ♥ Want their boundaries to be valued and recognized and safe

- ♥ Like to have a cupful of sharpened pencils, things in neat order

- ♥ Recognize patterns in nature

I Will Most Likely Do My Best Work...

...Planning Tomorrows
Lookabout Learners

- ❤ Learn by seeing and watching demonstrations
- ❤ Learn by reading, like descriptions and concentration
- ❤ Learn spelling, recognize words by sight
- ❤ Learn by writing, handwriting
- ❤ Are obedient when young
- ❤ Put things away when finished – do not like clutter
- ❤ Notice details, love knowledge
- ❤ Like to keep written records
- ❤ Put models together correctly using written directions
- ❤ Review for tests by writing a summary or reading notes
- ❤ Like a lot of eye contact
- ❤ Like "color" dressing, beautiful accessories, well-designed things

I Will Most Likely Do My Best Work...

...Inspiring Ideas

Talkabout Learners

Learn through verbal instructions from others or self

Enjoy dialogue and plays, often move lips or sub-vocalize

Like to talk a lot and are good storytellers

♥ Like to sing and enjoy music

Use mature language

♥ Learn telephone numbers and addresses quite young

Like to play with words and make up rhymes

♥ Are good dancers and drummers, have a good sense of rhythm

May talk to selves when working alone

Ask questions about written instructions

♥ Review for a test by reading aloud or reviewing with others

I Will Most Likely Do My Best Work...

...Tugging Hearts
Feelabout Learners

- ♥ Learn by doing, hands-on experiences
- ♥ Prefer stories where action occurs early
- ♥ Are often poor spellers
- ♥ Like to touch everything
- ♥ Make things out of paper
- ♥ Enjoy sports, are well-coordinated
- ♥ Like to take things apart and put them back together
- ♥ Are prone to fight rather than talk things out
- ♥ Like to draw and doodle, and enjoy art projects
- ♥ Are usually outdoors kind of people
- ♥ Spend time on crafts and shop-type activities
- ♥ Prefer movement games

I keep six honest serving men
(They taught me all I knew);
Their names are What and Why and When
And How and Where and Who.

— Rudyard Kipling

In describing a creation that organized itself, incorporating chaos and change into survival and progress, Darwin did not challenge the idea of God as the source of all being. But he did reject the idea of a God minutely implicated in every flaw and injustice and catastrophe. Darwin forced human beings to look at the inherent struggle of natural life head on, not as we wish it to be, but as it is in all its complexity and brutality and mystery. This is most difficult for human beings, perhaps in time of great change and turmoil such as ours in cultural moments of flux and global danger.

Chapter 12

Further Activities and Resources for Adults

Diversity and Putting Teamwork Together

Things to Do:
Putting Teamwork Together

Working with Diversity

How well do we live with diversity? We can help each other understand how our differences were designed to work together.

Gather quotes in a collection having to do with a child's world (learning, work, play, physical, spiritual, and emotional), then connect each quote with one of the four root values (order, understanding, freedom, and harmony).

List the things your child likes to spend time doing. These point to his or her most important values (plan a bike ride: order; ride a dirt bike: freedom; explore a new bike path: understanding; invite friends biking: harmony). Create something with photographs, paint, collage, sculpture, or in any material desired.

List the things a friend likes to spend time doing. Notice how different values can pull them both in opposite directions. Two people do not need the same values to have a good friendship. They must be able to support each other's values by negotiating their mutual needs.

Ask your child to think of a difficult time when he had the courage to go beyond what he or she thought was possible. Ask him to write a story about this time using the following sentence to start: I'm happier because this happened in my life, and I have a chance to learn that no experience is a bad experience, as long as I know how to learn something new from it.

What is your child's interpretation of *mad, glad,* and *sad,* or *would have, should have,* and *could have?*

Ask a group of children to find photos, tapes, drawings, or a thing that tells others something about them. Help them understand character, race, language, gender, customs, and background based on their own feedback. What do they think these things mean in our time?

In children, understanding creates respect for others who have different talents. Notice how one does something well that another has not yet learned. Ask them to compare old and new ideas of partnership.

Make a collage of a balance wheel of life, using six focus areas of physical, spiritual, play, relationship, work, education in any order. Notice how each spoke changes importance with need.

Things to Do: Putting Teamwork Together

Thinkabout Owl Activities
(Upper-left rectangle)

Ecology Issues — "Waste is a terrible thing to mind."

How does the Thinkabout Owl part of your thinking put ecological ideas to practical use? You might express sensitivity to the natural patterns in the outdoors, practical concern for our planet, a desire to help create plans for a better life for all. Example activity: Organize a recycle trash cleanup at the beach.

Lookabout Lion Activities
(Upper-right rectangle)

The Information Superhighway — "Planning ahead shows you have one."

How do Lookabout Lions provide vision and knowledge? How is the Global Village/information age ready for a change to a telecommunication system that seems logical? How does fear of change, economic uncertainty, and changing values set the stage for worldwide social change? Take this question as far as you can and make it age appropriate. Discuss how time is circular.

Talkabout Chimp Activities
(Lower-right rectangle)

The One Human Story repeats over and over
— "Listen; I have something to tell you!"

How does Talkabout Chimp's talking help? Does asking questions afflict the comfortable instead of comforting the afflicted? To educate for understanding, our experiences need to be relevant and informed. Answers become useful when we are able to talk about what hurts. How does reaching out to each other demonstrate that understanding our interconnectedness is key to solving the problems of the planet, on a personal level and on a global or collective level?

Feelabout Koala Activities
(Lower-left rectangle)

Interpersonal Psychology — "In action or in traction"

How do Feelabout Koalas perceive the physical body as fitness for living? Are beautiful people more worthy? We feel the beauty of a body, conscious of the collective needs on the planet. At the other end of the same line the anorexic girl self-consciously looks in the mirror and sees a fat girl. Discuss social values of body health.

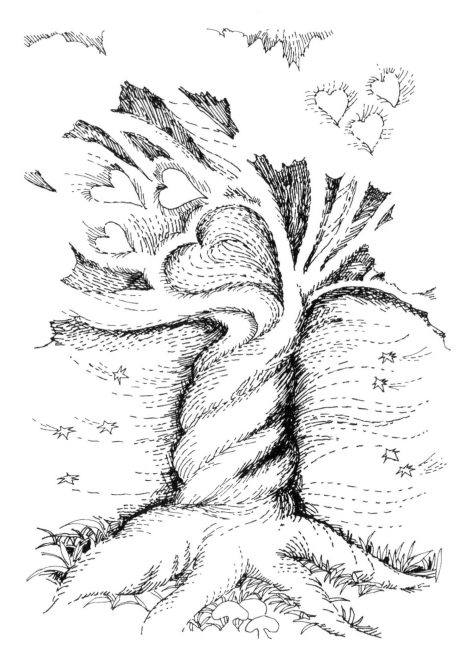

Friendship is a sheltering tree.

— **Samuel Taylor Coleridge**

Glossary for Caretakers

This glossary not only defines words used in special ways in this book but also adds additional, more technical words and explains how these concepts are portrayed in *Turning Points: Journey to Self Discovery*.

Adaptive—one's ability to adjust to circumstances; how the Synergy Pals work as a team to find appropriate methods to tackle problems in collaboration.

Affiliate—the need of people to associate with one another. In synergistic terms, learning to work harmoniously as a team, balancing tolerances and biases.

Anchor—A stimulus arising from experience, that when applied, elicits a specific response: pain or pleasure.

Anxiety—Vague apprehension or fear about the future.

Auditory—Using one's ears as the primary way to perceive the world and access information.

Away From—A preference to move in a reverse direction, away from pain, perceived as someone or something.

Belief—A general expectation or assumption about the way the world operates or other people behave. Beliefs are usually based on one's experience, temperament, and values. Beliefs are learned and can be unlearned or changed.

Chimp, Talkabout—A person who needs lots of "room" for ideas and creativity, to be able to share and discuss them with others whose opinions they value; and to feel understood on a really deep level. Perhaps, Talkabout Chimps might enjoy shaking things up a bit, possibly for shock value. See Explorer/Planner.

Common Ground—A level on which two people feel a personal connection, share a bond, a value, a belief, an experience, a feeling about a certain situation, a need, or a personality trait.

Communication—Exchanging information using verbal or written language and/or a variety of behavioral signals.

Content—The subject matter of events of life and/or interaction with others around which process happens.

Decision—The result of using the 7-step process to analyze and determine one's goals and plans for achievement. De-cide means to cut off, move away from pain to pleasure.

Detailer—A person with a natural talent for noticing, appreciating, planning for, and executing small, but often extremely important details.

Digital—Using language as the primary way to perceive the world and access information.

Disassociation—Having a memory without being connected with the feelings associated with the remembered experience.

Dream Mover—Someone who talks about the fun and inspired way to do things. See Chimp, Talkabout and Explorer/Planner.

Ecology—The study of how the individual affects the whole, the whole affects the individual, and the total relationship between an individual and his or her outer environment. Internal ecology is concerned with the relationship among one's own values, beliefs, expectations, and behavior toward unlimited potential.

Explorer—A person whose natural talents enable them to think out and consider new and different ways of accomplishing things.

Extrovert—One whose behavior is oriented more in an outward direction, toward other people and external circumstances, in alignment.

Freedom (Rhythms)—The space and lack of restrictions to make choices, whether traditional or adventurous; to think up and explore new and varied ideas; and to be boldly creative, without offending one's friends. Also, the space and opportunity to be one's self, who ever that may turn out to be.

Gestalt—The whole picture, the breadth and depth within which one usually focuses more narrowly. It is when one can see the "whole" that the "detail" can be kept in perspective

Harmony (Rhythms)—The peaceful co-existence of everyone concerned. It is not necessary for everybody to agree on every little thing for harmony to exist; however, it is absolutely necessary for each person to respect the opinions, feelings, ideas, needs, space, and values of everyone else involved.

Inertia—An impulse to remain in a given state, one's comfort zone, resulting in lack of challenge and growth.

Introvert—One who's behavior is oriented more in an inward direction, concerned with internal conditions.

Kinesthetic—Using one's feeling and touching senses as the primary way to perceive the world and access information.

Koala, Feelabout—A person who needs harmony, also, empathy, touching (hugs), and personal contact with friends and loved ones. It is extremely important to a Feelabout Koala to have a sense of belonging. Feelings, both his/her own, and those of others, will probably be a major motivating factor. See Nurturer.

Language—There are two levels of language: in addition to one's accustomed verbal means of communication (speaking and hearing words), language also refers to different individual "thinking languages," internal/mental communication, which may be visual, auditory, kinesthetic, or analytical.

Learning Styles—An individual's preferred means of acquiring and remembering new information (see Auditory, Digital, Kinesthetic, and Visual).

Lion, Lookabout—A big-picture person who needs options and choices, as well as challenges, and is driven to get results; a visionary, a free spirit. See Planner/Explorer.

Map—See Paradigm.

Matcher/Matching—Comparing input with known information to determine if it is harmonious or not.

Metaphor—A story that conveys a deeper meaning, that symbolizes how something works or what it means. The "Synergy Tree" story is a metaphor.

Order (Rhythms)—The sense of calm that can result from having a place for everything and everything in that place, as well as, having a schedule, a rhythm, to one's day or a particular project.

Owl, Thinkabout—A person who needs to feel safe, who needs to know the facts about a project or situation, who is most comfortable when things are done in an orderly fashion in an environment where everything is in its place, and one who notices, as well as provides, details. See Detailer.

Nurturer—A person with a natural talent for soothing and encouraging others.

Paradigm—A map, framework, or pattern on which to base a belief system. For example, the world was once thought to be flat and then known to be round: the change in how one thought about the shape of the world was a paradigm shift.

Part—A portion of one's personality—for example, the "parts" of Thinkabout Owl, Talkabout Chimp, Feelabout Koala, and Lookabout Lion within each individual.

Peacemaker—Someone who feels along for an easier way to do things. See Koala, Feelabout and Nurturer.

Planner—A person whose natural talents enable him to be prepared for both advantages and snags that might develop in a given situation, and deal with them efficiently, rather then being surprised and totally defeated.

Process—The growing, changing, evolving that happens around the content of events and interaction with others.

Rapport—The sense of trust, compatibility, and harmony established between people.

Representational Systems—The five senses (sight, hearing, touch, smell, taste) used to convey information to the brain.

Skill Master—Someone who thinks about which is the correct way to do things. See Owl, Thinkabout and Detailer.

State—The sum total of what one thinks, feels, and does at any given time. How emotions are managed may be dependent upon the circumstances of the moment.

Synergy—The effect of how interaction of heterogeneous parts multiplies the whole, which becomes more than just the sum of the parts. All life is related; each of us is connected to one another, unique, yet more alike than different; a partnership.

Temperament—One's natural method of action or behavior based on personality parts; for example, an individual may behave primarily as a Thinkabout Owl, but also have Talkabout Chimp, Lookabout Lion, and Feelabout Koala aspects to his or her behavior; feisty, fearful, feeling, or flexible are anthropomorphic metaphors.

Toward—A preference to move closer to pleasure associated with someone or something.

Understanding (Rhythms)—The ability not only to listen to someone, but also to hear and grasp what is being said; the ability to empathize, rather than just sympathize, with a friend or loved one's pain; to be able to feel rather than just observe.

Value—Principle held in high esteem against which people and events are measured as worthwhile or useless; for instance, Order, Freedom, Understanding, and Harmony are values, which if denied cause pain.

Vision Leader—Someone who looks around for a new way to do things. See Lion, Lookabout and Explorer/Planner.

Visual—Using ones eyes as the primary way to perceive the world and access information.

Discover How Your Child's Special Gifts Fit Well With Others

THE FRIENDLY UNIVERSE
C O L L E C T I O N

ISBN 0-9625385-6-6

ISBN 0-9625385-7-4

ISBN 0-9625385-8-2

ISBN 0-9625385-0-6

Find out with this New SQ Personality Quiz

Ardys Reverman, Ph.D., is internationally acclaimed as an innovative educator on the marvels and mysteries of the brain. Originally inspired by her own life as a Mom, her quest to understand innate talents add up to different ways of being smarter together. To learn more about her work and books go to: www.friendlyuniverse.com

For UG/Grad Course Registration Information www.friendlyuniverse.com

• SQ is not IQ — the latest brain science reveals, and research confirms, the importance of our synergy quotient.
• It's rewarding to discover your child's strengths — the earlier the better.
• All children learn differently, yet we tend to treat them as if they are the same.
• Help your child to understand and connect with others.
• We are all part of something larger than ourselves.
• Be smarter together for success in an uncertain world.
• A must read and DO to understand your personality.

These are wonderful Books that show you how to better understand and bring out the best in you and those who matter most in your life. The poems, illustrations and insights are powerful.

Brian Tracy, Ph.D.
author of No Excuses -The Power of Self Discipline

 Ardys Reverman PhD

drardy@friendlyuniverse.com www.friendlyuniverse.com or www.synergypals.com

Newly updated and revised editions available as a set

Recommended Reading

Armstrong, Thomas, Ph.D., *You're Smarter Than You Think: A Kid's Guide to Multiple Intelligences*. Free Spirit Publishing, 2003.

Bandler, Richard, Grinder, John, and Satir, Virginia, *Changing With Families*. Science and Behavior Books, 1976.

Bridges, William, *Managing Transitions: Making the Most of Change*. Da Capo Lifelong, 2009.

Buckingham Marcus and Clifton, Donald O., *Now Discover Your Strengths*. Free Press, 2001.

Burnham, Terry and Phelan, Jay, *Mean Genes*. Perseus Publishing, 2000.

Campbell, Joseph, *The Hero's Journey*. Harper & Row, 1990.

Carey, William B., *Understanding Your Child's Temperament*. MacMillan, 2005, 1997.

Gardner, Howard, *Five Minds for the Future*, Harvard Business Press, 2008.

Gladwell, Malcolm, *The Outliers: the Story of Success*. Little, Brown and Company, 2008.

Goleman, Daniel, *Emotional Intelligence*. Bantam Books, 1995.

Grandin, Temple, and Duffy, Kate, *Developing Talents: Careers for Individuals with Asperger Syndrome and High-Functioning Autism*. Shawnee Mission, KS: Autism Asperger Pub. Co., 2008.

Harris, Sam, *The Moral Landscape: How Science Can Determine Human Values*. Free Press, 2010.

Hartmann, Thomas, *Focus Your Energies*. Mythical Intelligence, 1994.

Gordon, Gary, *Building Engaged Schools: Getting the Most out of America's Classrooms*. The Gallup Organization, 2006.

Johansson, Frans, *Medici Effect: Breakthrough Insights at the Intersection of Ideas, Concepts & Cultures*. Harvard Business School Publishing, 2004.

Jung, Carl, *Psychological Types*. Pantheon, 1953.

Kandel, Eric R., *In Search of Memory: The Emergence of the New Science of Mind*. WW. Norton Company, 2006.

Keirsey, David, and Bates, Marilyn, *Please Understand Me: An Essay on Temperament Styles*. Prometheus Nemesis, 1978.

Kristal, Jan, *The Temperament Perspective: Working With Children's Behavioral Styles*. Brookes Publishing Co., 2005.

Levine, Mel, *A Mind at a Time*. Simon & Schuster, 2002.

Levitin, Daniel J., *The World in Six Songs*. Penguin Group, 2008.

Myers, Isabel Briggs with Peter B. Myers, *Gifts Differing: Understanding Personality Type*. Consulting Psychologists Press, 1995.

Neville, Helen and Diane Clark Johnson, *Temperament Tools: Working With Your Child's Inborn Traits*. Parenting Press, 1998.

Pink, Daniel H., *A Whole New Mind: Why Right-brainers Will Rule the Future*. Riverhead Books, 2005.

Pollan, Michael, *The Botany of Desire: A Plant's-Eye View of the World*. New York: Random House, 2002.

Reverman, Ardys, *In the Creative Circle*. Taproots Press, 1993.

Reverman, Ardys, *Teamwork is Child's Play*. Taproots Press, 1995.

Reverman, Ardys, *Team Smart SQ: Redefining What It Means to Be Smart*. Friendly Universe Collections, 2006.

Reverman, Ardys, *heart2heart: Be Yourself — Everyone Else Is Taken*. Friendly Universe Collections, 2011.

Reverman, Ardys, *Turning Points, Journey to Self Discovery*. Friendly Universe Collections, 2011.

Reverman, Ardys, *Treasure Quest, We Are Connected*. Friendly Universe Collections, 2011.

Robbins, Anthony, *Unlimited Power*. Simon and Schuster, 1986.

Robinson, Ken, Ph.D., *The Element: How finding Your Passion Changes Everything*. Viking, 2009.

Rosen, Sidney, *My Voice Will Go with You: The Teaching Tales of Milton H. Erickson, M.D.*. New York: Norton, 1982.

Rosenberg, Marshall B., Ph.D., *Nonviolent Communication, A Language of Life*. Puddle Dancer Press, 2003.

Russell, Peter, *The Global Brain*. J.P. Tarcher, 1983.

Satir, Virginia, *Your Many Faces: First Step to Being Loved*. CLArts, 1978.

Schiller Pam and Phipps Pat, *Starting with Stories: Engaging Multiple Intelligences*. Gryphon House, 2006.

Shaywitz, Sally, M.D., *Overcoming Dyslexia: a New and Complete Science-based Program for Reading Problems at Any Level*. Alfred A. Knopf, 2003.

Sloat, Donald E., PhD., *The Dangers of Growing Up in a Christian Home*. Thomas, Nelson Publishers, 1986.

Smith, Lendon H., *Hyper Kids*. Shaw/Spelling, 1990.

Strauss, William and Howe, Neil, *The Fourth Turning*. Broadway Books, 1997.

Tieger, Paul D. and Barbara Barron-Tieger, *Do What You Are*. Little Brown & Co., 1992.

Wiseman Rosalind, *Queen Bees and Wannabees*. Three Rivers Press, 2002.

Wood, Tracey, *Overcoming Dyslexia for Dummies*. Wiley Publishing, Inc., 2006.

Did you know that everybody is good at something? When we make our differences work together, that's heart2heart, a game of self-discovery.

iParenting Media
AWARDS

"I picked this game up for my nieces because I thought it looked like something they would enjoy. I've been told they absolutely LOVE to play this with their friends at sleep overs. If you're looking for a fun gift for your tweens, then this is it!"

The Role of Synergy in Our Brain's Common Senses

Playing **heart2heart** tells you a little about who you are and what makes your inner world unique. It helps you discover teamwork as you join your strengths with others to reach a goal. Thinking from the inside out, you experience a **new fun way** of self-discovery. You'll learn from the rest and be your best when you are part of the whole.

The **heart2heart game** by Discovery Bay Games uses **four colors** to describe personality. One color isn't better than any other. A mix of colors is normal, but you will tend to come up with some colors more often than others. Don't be surprised if your colors change at times, though. That's normal too. Four kinds of smart create a greater heart.

Red – Feel If you often come up with RED, you tend to make "friendly group" decisions based on feelings of harmony with those who matter most in your life.

Green – Think If you often come up with GREEN, it means you tend to make "careful dot-to-dot" decisions based on thinking about order, logic, facts and rules.

Yellow – Talk If you often come up with YELLOW, it means you tend to make "quick creative" decisions based on understanding and talking about new ideas.

Blue – Look If you often come up with BLUE, you tend to "take charge" of decisions in your own way. You look for vision in leadership.

**A new way of whole-brain learning
for the 21st century:
heart2heart game
for the family and classroom.**
Please order heart2heart today!

http://gifts.barnesandnoble.com/Toys-games/
Heart-To-Heart-Game/e/183338000499
Usually ships within 24 hours • UPC: 183338000499

http://www.amazon.com/Discovery-Bay-Games-1049-
Heart/dp/097918276X/ref=sr_1_12?ie=UTF8&s=toys-and-
games&qid=1280280529&sr=1-12

www.friendlyuniverse.com